The
Behavioral Medicine
Treatment Planner

PRACTICE *PLANNERS*™ SERIES

Treatment *Planners*

The Complete Adult Psychotherapy Treatment Planner
The Child and Adolescent Psychotherapy Treatment Planner
The Chemical Dependence Treatment Planner
The Continuum of Care Treatment Planner
The Couples Psychotherapy Treatment Planner
The Employee Assistance Treatment Planner
The Pastoral Counseling Treatment Planner
The Older Adult Psychotherapy Treatment Planner
The Behavioral Medicine Treatment Planner
The Family Psychotherapy Treatment Planner
The Group Therapy Treatment Planner
The Gay and Lesbian Psychotherapy Treatment Planner

Homework *Planners*

Brief Therapy Homework Planner
Brief Couples Therapy Homework Planner
Chemical Dependence Treatment Homework Planner
Brief Child Therapy Homework Planner
Brief Adolescent Therapy Homework Planner

Documentation *Sourcebooks*

The Clinical Documentation Sourcebook
The Forensic Documentation Sourcebook
The Psychotherapy Documentation Primer
The Chemical Dependence Treatment Documentation Sourcebook
The Clinical Child Documentation Sourcebook
The Couple and Family Clinical Documentation Sourcebook
The Clinical Documentation Sourcebook, 2e
The Continuum of Care Clinical Documentation Sourcebook

The
Behavioral Medicine
Treatment Planner

Douglas E. DeGood

Angela L. Crawford

Arthur E. Jongsma, Jr.

JOHN WILEY & SONS, INC.

New York • Chichester • Weinheim • Brisbane • Singapore • Toronto

Copyright © 1999 by Douglas DeGood, Angela L. Crawford, and Arthur E. Jongsma, Jr., Ph.D.
All rights reserved.
Published by John Wiley & Sons, Inc.
Published simultaneously in Canada.

All references to diagnostic codes and the entire content of Appendix B are reprinted with permission from the *Diagnostic and Statistical Manual of Mental Disorders, Fourth Edition.* Copyright 1994. American Psychiatric Association.

Library of Congress Cataloging-in-Publication Data
DeGood, Douglas E. (Douglas Earl), 1943–
    The behavioral medicine treatment planner / Douglas DeGood, Angela L. Crawford, and Arthur E. Jongsma, Jr.
        p.   cm. — (Practice planners series)
    Includes bibliographical references.
    ISBN 0-471-31926-0 (pbk./disk : alk. paper). — ISBN 0-471-31923-6 (pbk. : alk. paper)
    1. Medicine and psychology—Planning—Handbooks, manuals, etc.
    2. Mental illness—Treatment—Planning—Handbooks, manuals, etc.
    3. Psychiatric records—Handbooks, manuals, etc.   I. Crawford, Angela L.
    II. Jongsma, Arthur E., 1943–   . III. Title. IV. Series: Practice planners.
    [DNLM: 1. Behavioral Medicine handbooks.   2. Patient Care Planning handbooks. WB 39 D319b 1999]
    RC480.5.D44   1999
    616'.001'9—dc21
    DNLM/DLC
    for Library of Congress   99-13574
                                                                        CIP

Printed in the United States of America.

10 9 8 7 6 5 4 3 2

I dedicate this book to the memory of Timothy C. Toomey—a sorely missed friend, mentor, colleague, and contributor to the field of behavioral medicine.

Douglas E. DeGood

I dedicate this book to my parents, John and Neva Crawford, in appreciation for their love and support over the years.

Angela L. Crawford

I dedicate this book about the confluence of psychology and medicine to my daughter, Michelle L. Jongsma, an oncology nurse practitioner who provides sensitive emotional support and other powerful medicine to all of her patients at Georgia Cancer Specialists.

Arthur E. Jongsma, Jr.

CONTENTS

PRACTICE PLANNER SERIES PREFACE

The practice of psychotherapy has a dimension that did not exist 30, 20, or even 15 years ago—accountability. Treatment programs, public agencies, clinics, and even group and solo practitioners must now justify the treatment of patients to outside review entities that control the payment of fees. This development has resulted in an explosion of paperwork.

Clinicians must now document what has been done in treatment, what is planned for the future, and what the anticipated outcomes of the interventions are. The books and software in this Practice Planner series are designed to help practitioners fulfill these documentation requirements efficiently and professionally.

The Practice Planner series is growing rapidly. It now includes not only *The Complete Adult Psychotherapy Treatment Planner* and the *Child and Adolescent Psychotherapy Treatment Planner,* but also Treatment Planners targeted to specialty areas of practice, including: chemical dependency, the continuum of care, couples therapy, employee assistance, behavioral medicine, therapy with older adults, pastoral counseling, family therapy, group therapy, and more.

In addition to the Treatment Planners, the series also includes *TheraScribe®: The Computerized Assistant to Psychotherapy Treatment Planning* and *TheraBiller™: The Computerized Mental Health Office Manager,* as well as adjunctive books, such as the *Brief, Chemical Dependence, Couple, Child,* and *Adolescent Therapy Homework Planners, The Psychotherapy Documentation Primer,* and *Clinical, Forensic, Child, Couples and Family, Continuum of Care,* and *Chemical Dependence Documentation Sourcebooks*—containing forms and resources to aid in mental health practice management. The goal of the series is to provide practitioners with the resources they need in order to provide high-quality care in the era of accountability—or, to put it simply, we seek to help you spend more time on patients, and less on paperwork.

ARTHUR E. JONGSMA, JR.
Grand Rapids, Michigan

PREFACE

The enthusiastic response to *The Complete Adult Psychotherapy Treatment Planner* has triggered a series of books under the rubric of *Practice Planners,* published by John Wiley & Sons, Inc. Treatment Planner books have been written that focus on specific patient populations (e.g., chemical dependence, couples, adolescents, children) as well as those that focus on specific treatment modalities (e.g., family therapy, group therapy, continuum of care). To date, eight Treatment Planning books have been published, and six more (e.g., Neuropsychology, Gay and Lesbian) are in various stages of being written or produced. All of the Treatment Planner books can also be purchased with an optional companion electronic disk attached to the back of the book. These disks are designed to import the book data into *TheraScribe 3.0: The Computerized Assistant to Psychotherapy Treatment Planning. TheraScribe* is available as a separate product and allows for the computer generation of individualized treatment plans using the data from any of the Treatment Planner books. A companion office management software program, *TheraBiller,* is also now available to work in conjunction with *TheraScribe* or as a stand-alone product to produce patient and insurance billing. The Practice Planners also include several Documentation Sourcebooks and Psychotherapy Homework Planners. All of these books are designed to reduce the clinician's time spent on paperwork and increase time available for patient contact.

The application of interventions from the realm of cognitive-behavioral psychology to health care problems has been rapidly expanding over the past two decades. Such efforts now represent the primary patient load of many mental health clinicians. Our extensive personal experience with medical patients has led us to recognize a need for a *Behavioral Medicine Treatment Planner.* In most medical settings there is an expectation for rapid consultation—leading to an on-the-spot formulation of problems—leading to recommended interventions that can be immediately acted upon. In putting together this *Planner,* we found that it forced us to become more systematic and or-

ganized in carrying out a task that we were already doing. As an immediate bonus while writing this book we found it was becoming much
easier to fill out managed care insurance forms.

So we are pleased to introduce the *Behavioral Medicine Psychotherapy Treatment Planner*. This new *Planner* is slightly different from previous *Planners* in that it is organized by medical problems rather than
psychological/behavioral problems. However, like previous *Planners,* it
offers prewritten behavioral definitions, objectives, goals, and interventions, as well as diagnostic suggestions associated with the medical conditions. And like the prior volumes in this *Planner* series, it is designed
to stimulate thought, ease the paperwork crunch, and help clinicians develop treatment plans that meet the needs of managed care reviewers.

The pressing need for readable, efficient documentation that clearly
outlines assessment, treatment, progress, and discharge status cannot
be overemphasized when the mental health provider is part of an inter-
disciplinary treatment effort—which is nearly always the case for the
behavioral medicine clinician. As with the prior *Planners,* we have tried
to make our intervention recommendations eclectic in origin, spanning
the range from cognitive, behavioral, dynamic, familial, pharmacological, psychophysiological, educational, and didactic to bibliotherapeutic
and assessment oriented. It is our hope that the *Behavioral Medicine
Treatment Planner* will serve as a useful consultant, offering a wide variety of therapeutic ideas for your clinical consideration and streamlin-
ing the planning process.

In writing a book based on many years of professional experience,
we find that there are far too many influential mentors and colleagues
for us to thank individually. However, most of all, we would like to acknowledge the enthusiasm, courage, and gratitude of patients suffering
from pain, illnesses, and injuries that have encouraged and challenged
us to move our services from the mental health clinic directly into traditional inpatient and outpatient medical settings.

This *Behavioral Medicine Treatment Planner* has been developed
with the help of colleagues who have made themselves available for consultation, and we thank them for sharing their ideas. We also acknowledge the diligent work of Jennifer Byrne, who managed the manuscript
from scribbles to printed page. Finally, a word of thanks must be given
to Wiley editor Kelly Franklin, whose creative genius and faithful encouragement contribute greatly to the immense success of this Practice
Planner project.

> *Douglas E. DeGood*
> *Angela L. Crawford*
> *Arthur E. Jongsma, Jr.*

The
Behavioral Medicine
Treatment Planner

INTRODUCTION

Since the 1960s, formalized treatment planning has gradually become a vital aspect of the entire health care delivery system, whether it is treatment related to physical health, mental health, child welfare, or substance abuse. What started in the medical sector in the 1960s spread into the mental health sector in the 1970s as clinics, psychiatric hospitals, agencies, and so on, began to seek accreditation from bodies such as the Joint Commission on Accreditation of Healthcare Organizations (JCAHO) to qualify for third-party reimbursements. To achieve accreditation, most treatment providers had to begin developing and strengthening their documentation skills in the area of treatment planning. Previously, most mental health and substance abuse treatment providers had, at best, a "bare-bones" plan that looked similar for most of the individuals they treated. As a result, patients and third-party payers were uncertain about the direction of mental health treatment. Goals were vague, objectives were nonexistent, and interventions were not specific to individual patients. Outcome data were not measurable, and neither the treatment provider nor the patient knew exactly when treatment was complete. The initial development of rudimentary treatment plans made inroads toward addressing some of these issues.

With the advent of managed care in the 1980s, treatment planning has taken on even more importance. Managed care systems *insist* that clinicians move rapidly from assessment of the problem to the formulation and implementation of the treatment plan. The goal of most managed care companies is to expedite the treatment process by prompting the client and treatment provider to focus on identifying and changing behavioral problems as quickly as possible. Treatment plans must be specific as to the problems and interventions, individualized to meet the client's needs and goals, and measurable in terms of setting milestones that can be used to chart the patient's progress. Pressure from third-party payers, accrediting agencies, and other outside parties has therefore increased the need for clinicians to produce effective, high-quality treatment plans in a short time frame. However, many mental health care providers have little experience in treatment plan development. Our purpose in writing this book is to clarify, simplify, and accelerate the treatment planning process.

TREATMENT PLAN UTILITY

Detailed written treatment plans can benefit not only the patient, therapist, treatment team, insurance community, and treatment agency, but also the overall psychotherapy profession. The patient is served by a written plan because it stipulates the issues that are the focus of the treatment process. It is very easy for both provider and patient to lose sight of what the issues were that brought the client into therapy. This is especially true for the behavioral medicine patient who must learn to differentiate between the behavioral and the biological aspects of his or her symptoms and who may initially be confused as to the purpose of a referral to a mental health professional. The treatment plan is a guide that clarifies and structures the focus of the therapeutic contract. Since issues can change as therapy progresses, the treatment plan must be viewed as a dynamic document that can and must be updated to reflect any major change of problem, definition, goal, objective, or intervention.

Patients and therapists benefit from the treatment plan, which forces both to think about therapy outcomes. Behaviorally stated, measurable objectives clearly focus the treatment endeavor. Patients no longer have to wonder what therapy is trying to accomplish. Clear objectives also allow the patient to channel effort into specific changes that will lead to the long-term goal of problem resolution. Therapy is no longer a vague contract to just talk honestly and openly about emotions and cognitions until the patient feels better. Both patient and therapist are concentrating on specifically stated objectives using specific interventions.

Providers are aided by treatment plans because they are forced to think analytically and critically about therapeutic interventions that are best suited for objective attainment for the patient. Therapists were traditionally trained to "follow the client"—a model of intervention that does not work very well in a behavioral medicine setting, where the presenting symptoms are medical in nature. But now a formalized plan is the guide to the treatment process. The therapist must give advance attention to the particular approaches and techniques that will form the basis for the interventions. This much better fits the traditional medical concept of applying diagnostic specific treatment algorithms.

Clinicians benefit from clear documentation of treatment because it provides a measure of added protection from possible patient litigation. Malpractice suits are increasing in frequency, and insurance premiums are soaring. The first line of defense against allegations is a complete clinical record detailing the treatment process. A written, individualized, formal treatment plan that is the guideline for the therapeutic process, that has been reviewed and signed by the patient, and that is coupled with problem-oriented progress notes is a powerful defense against exaggerated or false claims.

A well-crafted treatment plan that clearly stipulates presenting problems and intervention strategies facilitates the treatment process carried out by team members in inpatient, residential, or intensive outpatient settings. Good communication between team members about what approach is being implemented and who is responsible for which intervention is critical. Team meetings to discuss client treatment used to be the only source of interaction between providers; often, therapeutic conclusions or assignment were not recorded. Now, a thorough treatment plan stipulates in writing the details of objectives and the varied interventions (e.g., pharmacological, milieu, group therapy, didactic, recreational, individual therapy) and who will implement them.

Every treatment agency or institution is constantly looking for ways to increase the quality and uniformity of the documentation in the clinical record. A standardized, written treatment plan with problem definitions, goals, objectives, and interventions in every patient's file enhances that uniformity of documentation. This uniformity eases the task of record reviewers inside and outside the agency. Outside reviewers, such as JCAHO, insist on documentation that clearly outlines assessment, treatment, progress, and discharge status.

The demand for accountability from third-party payers and health maintenance organizations (HMOs) is partially satisfied by a written treatment plan and complete progress notes. More and more managed care systems are demanding a structured therapeutic contract that has measurable objectives and explicit interventions. Clinicians cannot avoid this move toward being accountable to those outside the treatment process.

The psychotherapy profession stands to benefit from the use of more precise, measurable objectives to evaluate success in mental health treatment. With the advent of detailed treatment plans, outcome data can be more easily collected for interventions that are effective in achieving specific goals.

HOW TO DEVELOP A TREATMENT PLAN

The process of developing a treatment plan involves a logical series of steps that build on each other, much like constructing a house. The foundation of any effective treatment plan is the data gathered in a thorough biopsychosocial assessment. As the patient presents himself or herself for treatment, the clinician must sensitively listen to and understand what the client struggles with in terms of family-of-origin issues, current stressors, emotional status, social network, physical health, coping skills, interpersonal conflicts, self-esteem, and so on. Assessment data may be gathered from a social history, physical exam, clinical interview, psychological testing, or contact with a patient's significant others. The integration of the data by the clinician or the multidisciplinary treatment team members is critical for understanding the patient, as is an awareness of the basis of the patient's struggle. We have identified six specific steps for developing an effective treatment plan based on the assessment data.

Step One: Problem Selection

This *Planner* presents 26 common medical diagnoses and the behavioral/emotional problems frequently found to accompany these medical problems. The goals, objectives, and interventions may also be applicable to a wide range of other patients with related medical diagnoses. It is important to start with a thorough review of the patient's medical records, followed by obtaining the patient's view of his or her medical problem and its treatment. Next try to determine the degree and nature of the link between behavioral/emotional coping problems and the coexisting medical problems. Although the patient may discuss a variety of emotional/behavioral issues during the assessment, the clinician must ferret out the most significant problems on which to focus the treatment process. Usually a *primary* problem will surface, and *secondary* problems may also be evident. Some *other* problems may have to be set aside as not urgent enough to require treatment at this time. An effective treatment plan can only deal with a few selected problems, or treatment will lose its direction.

As the problems to be selected become clear to the clinician or the treatment team, it is important to include opinions from the patient as to his or her prioritization of issues for which help is being sought. A patient's motivation to participate in and cooperate with the treatment process depends, to some extent, on the degree to which treatment addresses his or her greatest needs.

Step Two: Problem Definition

Each individual patient presents with unique nuances how a problem behaviorally reveals itself in his or her life. Therefore, each problem that is selected for a psychological treatment focus requires a specific definition about how it is evidenced in the particular patient. The symptom pattern should be associated with diagnostic criteria and codes such as those found in the *Diagnostic and Statistical Manual* (DSM) or the *International Classification of Diseases.* (However, note that some third-party payers may require that the presenting medical diagnosis remain the primary diagnosis of record.) This *Planner,* following the pattern established by DSM-IV, offers such behaviorally specific definition statements to choose from or to serve as a model for your own personally crafted statements. You will find several behavioral symptoms or syndromes listed that may be associated with the 26 medical conditions.

Step Three: Goal Development

The next step in treatment plan development is that of setting broad goals for the resolution of the target problem. These statements need not be crafted in measurable terms but can be global, long-term goals that indicate a desired positive outcome to the treatment procedures. This *Planner* suggests several possible goal statements associated with each medical problem, but one statement is usually all that is required in a treatment plan.

Step Four: Objective Construction

In contrast to long-term goals, objectives must be stated in behaviorally measurable language. It must be clear when the patient has achieved the established objectives; therefore, vague, subjective objectives are not acceptable. Review agencies (e.g., JCAHO), HMOs, and managed care organizations insist that psychological treatment outcome be measurable. The objectives presented in this *Planner* are designed to meet this demand for accountability. Numerous alternatives are presented to allow construction of a variety of treatment plan possibilities for the same presenting problem. The clinician must exercise professional judgment as to which objectives are most appropriate for a given patient.

Each objective should be developed as a step toward attaining the broad treatment goal. In essence, objectives can be thought of as a series of steps that, when completed, will result in the achievement of the long-term goal. There should be at least two objectives for each problem, but the clinician may construct as many as are necessary for goal achievement. Target attainment dates may be listed for each objective.

New objectives should be added to the plan as the individual's treatment progresses. When all the necessary objectives have been achieved, the patient should have resolved the target problem successfully.

Step Five: Intervention Creation

Interventions are the actions of the clinician designed to help the patient complete the objectives. There should be at least one intervention for every objective. If the patient does not accomplish the objective after the initial intervention, new interventions should be added to the plan.

Interventions should be selected on the basis of the patient's needs and the treatment provider's full therapeutic repertoire. This *Planner* contains interventions from a broad range of therapeutic approaches, including cognitive, dynamic, behavioral, pharmacologic, family-oriented, and solution-focused brief therapy. Across the range of interventions the underlying focus centers on helping patients acquire emotional and behavioral skills for coping with the effects of pain, illness, and injury. Other interventions may be written by the provider to reflect his or her own training and experience. The addition of new problems, definitions, goals, objectives, and interventions to those found in the *Planner* is encouraged, because doing so adds to the database for future reference and use.

Some suggested interventions listed in the *Planner* refer to specific books that can be assigned to the patient for adjunctive bibliotherapy. Appendix A contains a full bibliographic reference list of these materials. The books are arranged under each medical condition for which they are appropriate as assigned reading for patients. When a book is used as part of an intervention plan, it should be reviewed with the patient after it is read, enhancing the application of the content of the book to the patient's specific circumstances. For further information about self-help books, mental health professionals may wish to consult *The Authoritative Guide to Self-Help Books* (1994) by Santrock, Minnett, and Campbell (available from The Guilford Press, New York). The Internet is also a rich source for locating information and self-help books, especially for recent publications (e.g., www.Amazon.com or Barnesandnoble.com).

Assigning an intervention to a specific provider is most relevant if the patient is being treated by a team (e.g., a pain-management program or cancer center) in an inpatient, residential, or intensive outpatient setting. Within these settings, personnel other than the primary clinician may be responsible for implementing a specific intervention. Review agencies may require that the responsible provider's name be stipulated for every intervention.

Step Six: Diagnosis Determination

In a behavioral medicine setting, even if the patient's primary diagnosis is a medical one, a psychological diagnosis usually must be provided if part of the treatment is to be behavioral in nature. The determination of an appropriate psychological diagnosis is based on an evaluation of the patient's complete clinical presentation. The clinician must compare the behavioral, cognitive, emotional, and interpersonal symptoms that the patient presents to the criteria for diagnosis of a mental illness condition as described in DSM-IV. The issue of differential diagnosis is admittedly a difficult one that research has shown to have rather low inter-rater reliability. Also, psychologists have been trained to think more in terms of maladaptive behavior than disease labels. In spite of these factors, diagnosis is a reality that exists in the world of mental health care and it is a necessity for third-party reimbursement. (However, managed care agencies have recently become more interested in behavioral indices exhibited by the patient than in the actual diagnosis.) It is the clinician's thorough knowledge of DSM-IV criteria and a complete understanding of the client assessment data that contribute to the most reliable, valid diagnosis. An accurate assessment of behavioral indicators will also contribute to more effective treatment planning.

HOW TO USE THIS PLANNER

Our experience has taught us that learning the skills of effective treatment plan writing can be a tedious and difficult process for many clinicians. It is even more stressful to develop this expertise when under the pressures of increased patient load and short time frames placed on clinicians today by managed care systems. The documentation demands can be overwhelming when we must move quickly from assessment to treatment plan to progress notes. In the process, we must be very specific about how and when objectives can be achieved, and how progress is exhibited in each client. *The Behavioral Medicine Treatment Planner* was developed as a tool to aid clinicians in writing a treatment plan in a rapid manner that is clear, specific, and highly individualized according to the following progression:

1. Based on referral information and patient's self-report, identify the presenting medical problem (Step One). Locate the corresponding page number for that problem (or a closely related problem) in the *Planner's* table of contents.
2. Select two or three of the listed behavioral definitions (Step Two) and record them in the appropriate section on your treatment

plan form. Feel free to add your own defining statement if you determine that your patient's behavioral manifestation of the identified medical problem is not listed.

3. Select a single long-term goal (Step Three) and again write the selection, exactly as it is written in the *Planner* or in some appropriately modified form, in the corresponding area of your own form.

4. Review the listed objectives for this problem and select the ones that you judge to be clinically indicated for your patient (Step Four). Remember, it is recommended that you select at least two objectives for each problem. You may add a target date or the number of sessions allocated for the attainment of each objective.

5. Choose relevant interventions (Step Five). The *Planner* offers suggested interventions related to each objective in the parentheses following the objective statement. But do not limit yourself to those interventions. The entire list is eclectic and may offer options that are more tailored to our theoretical approach or preferred way of working with patients. Also, just as with definitions, goals, and objectives, there is space allowed for you to enter your own interventions into the *Planner*. This allows you to refer to these entries when you create a plan around this problem in the future. You may assign responsibility to a specific person for implementation of each intervention if the treatment is being carried out by a multidisciplinary team.

6. Several DSM-IV diagnoses are listed at the end of each chapter that are commonly associated with a patient who has this type of problem. These diagnoses are meant to be suggestions for clinical consideration. Select a diagnosis listed or assign a more appropriate choice from the DSM-IV (Step Six).

Note: To accommodate those practitioners who tend to plan treatment in terms of diagnostic labels rather than presenting problems, Appendix B lists all the DSM-IV diagnoses that have been presented in the various presenting problem chapters as suggestions for consideration. Each diagnosis is followed by the presenting problems that have been associated with that diagnosis. The provider may look up the presenting problems for a selected diagnosis to review definitions, goals, objectives, and interventions that may be appropriate for their patients with that diagnosis.

Congratulations! You should now have a complete, individualized treatment plan that is ready for immediate implementation and presentation to the patient. It should resemble the format of the sample plan presented on page 10.

A FINAL NOTE

One important aspect of effective treatment planning is that each plan should be tailored to the individual patient's problems and needs. Treatment plans should not be mass-produced, even if patients have similar problems. The individual's strengths and weaknesses, unique stressors, social network, family circumstances, and symptom patterns *must* be considered in developing a treatment strategy. Drawing upon our own years of clinical experience, we have put together a variety of treatment choices. These statements can be combined in thousands of permutations to develop detailed treatment plans. Relying on their own good judgment, clinicians can easily select the statements that are appropriate for the individuals they are treating. In addition, we encourage readers to add their own definitions, goals, objectives, and interventions to the existing samples. It is our hope that the Treatment Planner will promote effective and creative treatment planning—a process that will ultimately benefit the patient, clinician, and medical community.

SAMPLE TREATMENT PLAN

Problem: ARTHRITIS

Definition: Severe disability in physical capacity due to joint pain
and stiffness.
Joint pain and stiffness are very stressful and lead to
depression, helplessness, and worry.

Goals: Maintain as many normal life activities as possible,
even if modifications are necessary.

Short-Term Objectives	Therapeutic Interventions
1. Maintain activities of daily living using strategies for coping with acute flare-ups as well as everyday symptoms.	1. Make sure patient understands how medication is to be taken. Explain use of compliance aids such as calendars and special packaging. 2. Make referral to occupational therapist for help with performing activities of daily living.
2. Engage in daily exercise program designed to increase joint flexibility and strengthen muscles for joint support.	1. Make referral to physical therapist for help in establishing joint-specific and general exercise program. 2. Encourage adherence to exercise regimen prescribed by physician and/or physical therapist.
3. Practice breath control and deep-muscle relaxation as a means of symptom management.	1. Instruct patient in how to use both brief, quick physical relaxation strategies (e.g., deep breathing, muscle tension release) and deeper, more time-intensive strategies (e.g., deep-muscle relaxation, guided imagery, hand warming). 2. Administer biofeedback to help patient identify physical signs of tension and learn to counter with self-relaxation skills.

Diagnosis: 316   Psychological Factors Affecting Arthritis

ACUTE PAIN

BEHAVIORAL DEFINITIONS

1. Pain of recent onset or short duration that is phasic or continuous and is often associated with autonomic activity typical of the emergency "fight-or-flight" anxiety response.
2. Autonomic hyperactivity revealed by palpitations, sweating, shallow breathing, shortness of breath, dry mouth, trouble swallowing, or nausea.
3. Motor tension as evidenced by restlessness, tiredness, shakiness, or muscle tension.
4. Hypervigilance as evidenced by feeling on edge, difficulty with attention and concentration, trouble falling or staying asleep, and generalized irritability.
5. Avoidance of seeking proper diagnostic evaluation and treatment for suspected medical or dental condition because of fear of pain.
6. Slowing of the healing process following onset of illness or injury, due to physical and emotional reaction to pain.
7. Pain-related behaviors (e.g., moaning, groaning, wincing, restlessness) that are disturbing to others who witness them.
8. Frequent complaints regarding treatment due to high degree of discomfort.

__. _____
   _____
__. _____
   _____
__. _____
   _____

LONG-TERM GOALS

1. Reduce and control severity of pain and emotional suffering.
2. Increase cognitive-behavioral skills for coping with acute pain and reduce feelings of helplessness.
3. Limit impact of pain on daily functions.
4. Reduce and control fear and irrational thinking in anticipation and response to pain.
5. Eliminate avoidance of necessary medical or dental procedures because of fear of anticipated pain associated with those procedures.

—. _____

_____

—. _____

_____

—. _____

_____

SHORT-TERM OBJECTIVES

1. Describe physical discomfort and express fears about pain. (1, 2, 3)
2. Verbalize beliefs regarding the role of pain in the present medical condition. (4)
3. State the level of pain that can be tolerated (on a scale of 1 to 10) and still function reasonably. (5)
4. Describe how pain affects daily life. (6)
5. List pain-coping mechanisms that have been used and describe their degree of success. (7)
6. Describe the use (and any abuse) of pain medications. (8, 9)

THERAPEUTIC INTERVENTIONS

1. Probe history of physical pain and its causes.
2. Encourage the patient to describe fears about present and future pain.
3. Encourage the patient to describe past painful trauma, illness, or medical procedure experiences that may be the basis of current fears.
4. Explore the patient's understanding, expectations, and beliefs regarding the role of pain in his/her medical condition.
5. Encourage the patient to verbalize feelings or beliefs about what is a tolerable level of discomfort.

7. Use medication as pre-scribed and report benefits and problems to therapist and doctors. (8, 9, 10)

8. Cooperate with a referral to a pain management team. (11)

9. Actively seek out information that can help with understanding source of pain (e.g., learn what to expect from illness, injury, or medical procedures). (12)

10. Verbalize an understanding of the benefits of cognitive interventions in building tolerance to pain. (13)

11. Identify negative self-talk that builds tension, anxiety, and fear resulting in exacerbation of pain. (14)

12. Verbalize an understanding of the relationship between acute pain and emotions, especially anxiety. (14, 15)

13. Use cognitive strategies (e.g., recognizing and controlling catastrophic thinking) that can reduce or eliminate the irrational fear component of pain. (13, 16, 17, 19)

14. Implement psychophysiologic self-relaxation and self-analgesia skills that can reduce physiologic reaction and increase tolerance of pain. (18, 19)

15. Practice pairing self-relaxation with visualization of remaining calm during medical or dental procedures. (19, 20)

6. Ask the patient to list the negative ways pain has interfered with normal functioning.

7. Assist the patient in defining what coping mechanisms have been used (e.g., taking more medication, social withdrawal, pacing, complaining, going to bed) and probe the degree of success for each in dealing with pain.

8. Review the patient's drug regimen for managing pain. If needed, discuss with physician possible changes in pain medication.

9. Assess patient for the practice of abusing pain medications and for the possible existence of chemical dependence.

10. Help the patient articulate satisfaction and/or dissatisfaction with balance between medication-produced analgesia and side effects.

11. Discuss with the patient and primary care physician the benefit of a consultation with pain management team.

12. Prepare the patient for painful medical procedures by discussing what to expect. Recognize individual differences—not all patients desire and benefit equally from detailed preparatory information.

16. Modify behavior to accommodate to pain (e.g., learn and use proper body mechanics for lifting and reaching). (21, 22, 25)

17. Verbalize acceptance of the need for vocational or marital/family counseling to deal with maladaptive responses to pain. (23)

18. Identify appropriate circumstances to ask for help from others versus circumstances that should be dealt with independently. (24)

19. Use physical aids to ease pain. (25)

20. Verbalize adaptive philosophic and spiritual attitudes toward pain and suffering as sometimes a necessary part of life. (26, 27)

21. Implement successful pain coping thoughts and/or behaviors from the past to promote functioning and increased pain tolerance in the present circumstance. (7, 28)

__. _____
   _____

__. _____
   _____

__. _____
   _____

13. Use examples (e.g., discussion of natural childbirth preparation) to illustrate the value of cognitive-behavioral interventions in aiding with tolerance of acute pain.

14. Assist the patient in identifying automatic thoughts that lead to fear and anxiety associated with actual or anticipated pain.

15. Teach the patient to recognize the overlap between acute pain and anxiety.

16. Help the patient identify healthy self-talk as a means of reducing the pain related to anxiety.

17. Teach the patient to use pleasant mental images along with self-relaxation to focus attention away from pain.

18. Instruct the patient in the use of psychophysiologic self-relaxation skills (i.e., slow deep breathing, muscle relaxation, hand warming) for reducing pain and emotional reactions to pain.

19. Instruct the patient in covert cognitive rehearsal (e.g., imagine viewing oneself using self-relaxation and other coping skills) during painful medical procedure.

20. Encourage and reinforce the use of relaxation skills during medical procedures to reduce anxiety.

21. Discuss with the patient the concept of "good" versus "bad" pain (e.g., in conjunction with postsurgical or postinjury fear of activity).

22. Counsel the patient concerning practical issues (e.g., movement, shifting position) with trauma or postoperative pain. Refer to occupational therapist for practical suggestions.

23. Assess the need for vocational or marital/family counseling to promote resolution of conflicts that result from patient's response to pain and refer if necessary.

24. Review the patient's attitudes about asking for help from others; encourage striking of balance between seeking out necessary aid, and avoiding excessive dependence and helplessness.

25. Discuss positive and negative attitudes toward the use of physical aids (e.g., wheelchairs, crutches); encourage attitudes that promote safer functioning.

26. Teach the patient the concept of pain as a normal, necessary part of life that ebbs and flows with all people at all times.

27. Support the patient in use of spiritual practices that bring a sense of peace in the face of pain.

28. Using a brief therapy technique, identify what pain-coping mechanism may have worked in the past to build tolerance and promote the continuation of normal functioning; encourage and reinforce its implementation now.

__. _____
    _____

__. _____
    _____

__. _____
    _____

DIAGNOSTIC SUGGESTIONS

Axis I:	307.89	Pain Disorder Associated with Both Psychological Factors and (Axis III Disorder)
	316	Psychological Factors Affecting (Axis III Disorder)
	300.29	Specific Phobia
	308.3	Acute Stress Disorder
	309.81	Posttraumatic Stress Disorder
	_____	_____
	_____	_____

ANXIETY RELATED TO MEDICAL PROBLEMS

BEHAVIORAL DEFINITIONS

1. Fear about medical condition or prognosis that causes significant distress and/or interferes with daily functioning.
2. Excessive and persistent fear associated with the occurrence or anticipation of specific medical procedures or treatments.
3. Anxiety, fear, or worry that exacerbates physical symptoms of medical disorder (e.g., pain, breathing difficulties, cardiac symptoms).
4. Excessive and persistent daily worry about several life circumstances.
5. Symptoms of motor tension such as restlessness, fatigue, shakiness, or muscle tension.
6. Symptoms of autonomic hyperactivity such as palpitations, shortness of breath, dry mouth, trouble swallowing, nausea, or diarrhea.
7. Symptoms of hypervigilance such as constantly feeling on edge, concentration difficulties, trouble falling or staying asleep, and general state of irritability.

—. _____
   _____
   _____
—. _____
   _____
   _____
—. _____
   _____

LONG-TERM GOALS

1. Increase accurate knowledge about medical condition—resulting in decreased irrational, anxiety-producing beliefs about symptoms, prognosis, and treatment.

2. Enhance ability to effectively manage fears and worry about medical condition.
3. Develop effective coping strategies to reduce anxiety during feared medical procedures.
4. Reduce overall level, frequency, and intensity of anxiety so that daily functioning is not impaired.
5. Stabilize anxiety level while increasing ability to function on a daily basis.
6. Resolve the core conflict that is the source of anxiety.

__. _____
   _____
__. _____
   _____
__. _____
   _____

SHORT-TERM OBJECTIVES

1. Describe history of anxiety, including associated symptoms, precipitating factors (if applicable), and strategies used to resolve it. (1, 2, 3)

2. Verbalize fears about medical disorder, prognosis, and treatment procedures. (4, 5)

3. Verbalize thoughts and feelings about deterioration of health and fears of death. (4, 5)

4. Identify major life conflicts from the past and present. (6, 7)

5. Verbalize insight into how past traumatic experiences are causing anxiety in present unrelated circumstances. (8)

THERAPEUTIC INTERVENTIONS

1. Develop rapport and trust with patient in order to create a supportive environment that will facilitate describing fears.

2. Obtain a history of patient's anxiety, including any precipitating factors and ways he/she has attempted to resolve it.

3. Assess the cognitive, behavioral, and somatic symptoms associated with anxiety episodes.

4. Explore anxiety and fear associated with medical condition and its treatment.

5. Explore and process patient's fears about deterioration of health, death, and dying.

6. Develop and implement relaxation and diversion strategies to reduce anxiety. (9, 10, 11)

7. Complete assigned homework focused on stress-reduction techniques. (12)

8. Create a hierarchy of anxiety-provoking medical procedures and cooperate with systematic desensitization procedures to reduce anxiety. (13, 14)

9. Identify how worries are irrational. (15)

10. Increase understanding of beliefs and cognitions that produce worry and anxiety. (16, 17)

11. Decrease level of anxiety by developing positive, calming self-talk. (17, 18)

12. Verbalize an understanding of the role that anxiety symptoms play in exacerbating medical problems. (19)

13. Utilize thought-stopping technique to interrupt anxiety-producing thoughts. (20)

14. Identify alternative positive views that are incompatible with anxiety-producing views. (21)

15. Increase knowledge about medical disorder. (22)

16. Verbalize enhanced self-efficacy and a sense of control in managing medical condition. (22, 23, 24)

6. Ask patient to develop a list of significant past and present life conflicts.

7. Assist patient in becoming aware of unresolved life conflicts and in starting to work toward their resolution.

8. Help patient develop insight into the link between past emotional issues and current anxiety.

9. Teach patient to utilize guided imagery to reduce anxiety.

10. Train in progressive muscle relaxation and diaphragmatic breathing to reduce physiological reactivity.

11. Utilize biofeedback training to facilitate relaxation skills.

12. Assign or allow patient to choose a chapter in *Relaxation and Stress Reduction Workbook* (Davis, Robbins-Ehelan, and McKay) and then work with him/her to implement the chosen technique.

13. Assist patient in developing a hierarchy of feared situations.

14. Utilize systematic desensitization to decrease anxiety during aversive medical procedures and other feared situations.

15. Assist patient in analyzing fears by examining the probability of the negative event occurring, the ability

17. Verbalize reasonable, factually-based information regarding medical condition, treatment, and prognosis. (4, 19, 22, 25)

18. Attend a support group for medical disorder and process impact of attending with therapist. (26)

19. Implement strategies to enhance sense of control in coping with daily stressors. (27)

20. Maintain regular exercise regimen as recommended by physician. (28)

21. Identify an anxiety-coping mechanism that has been successful in the past and increase its use. (29)

22. See physician for physical examination to assess need for medications and to rule out physical causes of anxiety. (30)

23. Take medications as prescribed and report side effects to appropriate professionals. (31)

—. _____

    _____

—. _____

    _____

—. _____

    _____

to control the event, the worst possible outcome, and the ability to accept the event (see *Anxiety Disorders and Phobias* by Beck and Emery).

16. Explore cognitive messages that mediate patient's anxiety.

17. Utilize cognitive restructuring to help patient develop reality-based, positive cognitions that enhance self-confidence in coping with fears.

18. Reinforce patient's implementation of positive coping thoughts to reduce anxiety and promote self-efficacy in feared situations.

19. Educate patient about the role of anxiety in exacerbating physical symptoms associated with medical disorder (e.g., pain, breathing difficulties, cardiac symptoms).

20. Teach patient to implement thought-stopping techniques to decrease obsessive ruminations (e.g., visualizing a stop sign each time the thought occurs, and then imagining a pleasant scene).

21. Reframe the fear by offering alternative ways of viewing the feared situation or enlarging the perspective.

22. Assist patient in acquiring information about medical disorder from books and

medical personnel in order to enhance sense of control and to challenge irrational beliefs or fears.

23. Encourage patient to take an active role in medical treatment decision making.

24. Reinforce patient's assertiveness in seeking information, expressing needs, and sharing feelings and concerns with medical professionals.

25. Help patient identify and challenge irrational beliefs about health status, medical treatment, and prognosis that exacerbate anxiety.

26. Assign patient to attend a support group related to his/her medical disorder.

27. Assist patient in developing coping skills (e.g., time management, communication skills, and problem solving) to manage stressful situations.

28. Encourage medically appropriate exercise regimen.

29. Using a brief solution-focused therapy approach, identify and clarify a time or situation in which patient managed anxiety adaptively; encourage patient to increase use of this strategy, modifying the solution as required.

30. Refer to physician for medication consultation and to rule out medical causes of anxiety.

31. Monitor medication compli-
    ance, side effects, and effec-
    tiveness. Confer with
    physician regularly.

___. _____

    _____

___. _____

    _____

___. _____

    _____

DIAGNOSTIC SUGGESTIONS

Axis I: 309.24   Adjustment Disorder with Anxiety
          300.29   Specific Phobia
          300.02   Generalized Anxiety Disorder
          293.89   Anxiety Disorder Due to (Axis III Disorder)
          300.00   Anxiety Disorder NOS
          307.89   Pain Disorder Associated with Both
                   Psychological Factors and (Axis III Disorder)
          316   Psychological Factors Affecting (Axis III
                   Disorder)

          _____   _____

          _____   _____

ARTHRITIS

BEHAVIORAL DEFINITIONS

1. Pain, stiffness, and swelling in the joints.
2. Disease process began in adulthood and has worsened with aging.
3. Severe disability in physical capacity due to joint pain and stiffness.
4. Joint pain and stiffness are very stressful and lead to depression, feelings of helplessness, and worry.

—. _____

_____

—. _____

_____

—. _____

_____

LONG-TERM GOALS

1. Maintain as many normal life activities as possible, even if modifications are necessary.
2. Utilize exercise as much as possible to maintain joint and muscle functioning.
3. Strengthen emotional and problem-solving abilities and acquire good stress- and pain-management skills.
4. Change activities and living arrangements as required to accommodate age and disease process.
5. Acquire needed information about living with arthritis.
6. Make maximum use of community resources to help maintain functional independence.

7. Develop effective partnerships with health care providers.

—. _____

_____

—. _____

_____

—. _____

_____

SHORT-TERM OBJECTIVES

1. Verbalize confidence in adequacy of doctor's workup and advice for management of arthritis. (1, 2)

2. Verbalize understanding of the causes and control of arthritis symptoms. (2, 3)

3. Use social support network effectively (e.g., family, church, friends, social services, medical services, educational and recreational resources). (4, 5)

4. Verbalize alternative activity and living arrangement plans that can be implemented if capacity for independent living should deteriorate. (5, 6, 8)

5. Adhere to plan for medication use. (7, 8)

6. Maintain activities of daily living using strategies for coping with acute flare-ups as well as everyday symptoms. (7, 8, 9)

THERAPEUTIC INTERVENTIONS

1. Discuss patient's satisfaction with current arthritis medical care and overall symptoms management plan.

2. Provide discussion and reading material (e.g., *Arthritis 101: Questions You Have, Answers You Need* by Arthritis Foundation, or *The Arthritis Helpbook* by Lorig and Fries) regarding nature and regulation of arthritis.

3. Assist patient in understanding difference between osteoarthritis and rheumatoid arthritis.

4. Inform patient of available resources, including arthritis support group.

5. Encourage patient and family to create a contingency plan (e.g., assisted living or home-bound assistance) for use if physical condition should deteriorate.

7. Cooperate with weight-loss regimen to reduce pressure on joints. (10)

8. Engage in daily exercise program designed to increase joint flexibility and strengthen muscles for joint support. (11, 12)

9. Verbalize feelings of depression associated with arthritis disease process. (13, 14)

10. Verbalize an understanding of the role of stress in exacerbating arthritis symptoms. (15, 16)

11. Identify sources of stress that cause muscle tension. (16, 17)

12. Identify and implement environmental changes that will reduce stress. (4, 16, 17, 18)

13. Verbalize an understanding of how mood may contribute to or result from arthritis symptoms. (15, 19, 24)

14. Identify negative self-talk that precipitates dysfunctional emotional responses. (20, 21, 24)

15. Implement positive self-talk in response to daily stressors. (21, 22)

16. Report a reduction in irritability with significant others. (18, 19, 20, 23)

17. Verbalize an understanding of how behavioral coping strategies can aid in pain management. (24)

6. Assist patient in identifying physical deficits that may impair independence now or in the future.

7. Make sure patient understands how medication is to be taken. Explain use of compliance aids such as calendars and special packaging.

8. Monitor use of medication for effectiveness and side effects, assessing for any abuse of painkilling medication.

9. Make referral to occupational therapist for help with performing activities of daily living.

10. Develop, implement, and monitor a weight-loss program to reduce strain on joints. (See chapter on Obesity in this *Planner.*)

11. Make referral to physical therapist for help in establishing joint-specific and general fitness exercise program.

12. Encourage adherence to exercise regimen prescribed by physician and/or physical therapist.

13. Assess for coexisting clinical depression through interview and/or testing instruments. (See Depression chapter in this *Planner.*)

14. Process feelings of grief over lost abilities and activities.

18. Practice breath control and deep-muscle relaxation as a means of symptom management. (25, 26, 27, 28, 29)

__. _____
_____

__. _____
_____

__. _____
_____

15. Teach patient how muscle tension and stress can exacerbate the negative effects of arthritis.

16. Assist patient in recognizing sources of environmental stress.

17. Discuss with patient cognitive and physical condition of spouse and any others that may be living in family household and causing stress to patient.

18. Assist patient in identifying changes that can be made in life to reduce stress.

19. Teach ways to recognize emotional responses to pain and physical limitations that may contribute to increased pain and physical limitations.

20. Assist patient in identifying the distorted schema and related automatic thoughts that mediate muscle tension, anxiety, irritability, and increased physical discomfort.

21. Help patient recognize how negative distorted cognitions (e.g., overgeneralization, catastrophizing) can generate negative self-talk, and negative self-talk can exaggerate a stressor's impact, triggering more tension and pain.

22. Teach and reinforce positive, realistic, cognitive self-talk as a means of coping

with stressors more effectively.

23. Help patient recognize how pain may reduce emotional control, thus leading to interpersonal conflicts. Assist patient in how to avoid venting frustration on others.

24. Aid patient in understanding the integration of cognitive-behavioral coping skills with an appropriate medical plan.

25. Train patient in use of psychophysiologic self-relaxation techniques (i.e., focused attention, mental imagery, muscle relaxation, hand warming, sensory alteration).

26. Administer biofeedback to help patient identify physical signs of tension and learn to counter with self-relaxation skills.

27. Instruct patient in how to use both brief, quick physical relaxation strategies (e.g., deep breathing, muscle tension release) and deeper, more time-intensive strategies (e.g., deep-muscle relaxation, guided imagery, hand warming).

28. Recommend books on relaxation techniques (e.g., *The Relaxation Response* by Benson, or *The Relaxation and Stress Reduction Workbook* by Davis, Eshelman, and McKay).

29. Assess patient's special difficulty with focusing attention, feelings of vulnerability, parasympathetic rebound, or excessive self-criticism, providing appropriate remediation.

__. _____

_____

__. _____

_____

__. _____

_____

DIAGNOSTIC SUGGESTIONS

Axis I:	316	Psychological Factors Affecting Arthritis
	V61.9	Relational Problem Related to a Mental Disorder or Arthritis
	V71.09	No Diagnosis or Condition on Axis I
	V62.89	Phase of Life Problem
	V15.81	Noncompliance with Treatment
	310.1	Personality Change Due to Arthritis
	_____	_____
	_____	_____

ASTHMA

BEHAVIORAL DEFINITIONS

1. Periodic episodes of wheezing, dyspnea, chest tightness, choking sensation, and cough.
2. Feelings of anxiety associated with asthma symptoms or anticipation of asthma symptoms.
3. Chronic asthma symptoms that interfere with daily activities or restrict quality of life.
4. Worry about future asthma attacks that causes hesitancy in planning or engaging in activities or exercise.
5. Fear of asthma symptoms (e.g., breathing difficulties) that contributes to hyperventilation and increased autonomic arousal.
6. Psychological (e.g., anxiety, psychosocial stressors) or behavioral (e.g., cigarette smoking, lack of compliance with medical treatment) factors that exacerbate asthma symptoms and/or trigger asthma attacks.
7. Emotional distress and coping difficulties associated with chronic asthma.

__. _____
_____

__. _____
_____

__. _____
_____

LONG-TERM GOALS

1. Prevent asthma attacks from occurring when possible and minimize intensity of asthma exacerbations when they can't be prevented.
2. Increase sense of control and self-efficacy in managing asthma.
3. Reduce fear, anxiety, and worry associated with asthma symptoms.
4. Improve quality of life and reduce disruption in daily activities caused by asthma.
5. Acquire stress-management skills to enhance emotional adaptation to asthma.
6. Identify and change psychological or behavioral factors that exacerbate asthma symptoms.

—. _____

   _____

—. _____

   _____

—. _____

   _____

SHORT-TERM OBJECTIVES

1. Describe medical condition and treatment regimen to the extent they are understood. (1)

2. Verbalize increased knowledge about asthma and treatment options. (2, 3)

3. Comply with medical treatment regimen, reporting any side effects or problems to appropriate medical personnel. (4, 5, 6, 7)

4. Summarize the plan for ongoing medical care. (7)

THERAPEUTIC INTERVENTIONS

1. Ask patient to provide a history of asthma condition. Assess patient's level of understanding of treatment regimen, asthma triggers, and prognosis.

2. Consult with patient's physician to enhance coordination of medical and behavioral treatments for asthma.

3. Assist patient in obtaining information about asthma and its treatment from sources such as physicians, the American Lung Associa-

5. Report to physicians or therapists any physical symptoms that cause concern. (7, 8, 9)

6. Increase assertiveness in interacting with health care professionals to enhance a sense of control in managing asthma. (9, 10)

7. Verbalize increased knowledge about the physiology of respiration and potential asthma triggers. (11, 13, 15)

8. Increase awareness of asthma triggers by keeping a journal of environmental, emotional, and psychosocial factors associated with asthma exacerbations. (12, 13)

9. Make changes in environment to reduce exposure to asthma triggers. (14, 25, 32)

10. Practice relaxation techniques on a daily basis to relieve tension, reduce physiological arousal, and enhance coping with daily stressors. (15, 16, 17)

11. Develop a hierarchy of anxiety-provoking symptoms or situations and participate in systematic desensitization procedures to reduce anxiety associated with asthma. (18, 19)

12. Utilize peak-flow meter to identify onset of asthma exacerbations and as a guide to taking medication or en-

tion, and the Asthma and Allergy Foundation.

4. Monitor and reinforce patient's compliance with medical treatment regimen. Utilize behavioral contracting to increase compliance as indicated.

5. Explore and address misconceptions, fears, and situational factors that contribute to lack of compliance with treatment regimen.

6. Assist patient in developing strategies to enhance adherence to medication regimen (e.g., self-monitoring of medication use, prompts from significant others, reminder beepers).

7. Encourage and reinforce regular contact with medical personnel to address questions regarding asthma symptoms, medications, and side effects and to develop an ongoing plan of treatment.

8. Assist patient in identifying those physical symptoms that require immediate medical attention and review the necessary steps to obtain appropriate medical care.

9. Encourage and reinforce patient's assertiveness in asking questions, expressing needs, describing symptoms, and sharing feelings with medical personnel and significant others.

gaging in appropriate self-management strategies. (20, 21)

13. Utilize support system to implement asthma management strategies and to facilitate coping with chronic illness. (22, 25, 26)

14. Develop and implement a plan for smoking cessation involving all smokers in the household. (23, 24)

15. Attend an asthma support group and discuss emotional reactions with therapist. (26)

16. Identify and verbally express emotions associated with medical condition and disruption in daily functioning. (25, 26, 27, 28, 29)

17. List circumstances in life that lead to worry and tension, and identify those that can be altered to reduce stress and dissatisfaction. (30, 31)

18. Implement changes in life situation (e.g., social, familial, vocational, recreational) to reduce level of stress. (31, 32)

19. Identify negatively distorted, irrational beliefs about medical condition and symptoms. (33, 35)

20. Replace negative cognitions with more realistic messages that promote a positive outlook. (34, 35, 36)

10. Use modeling, role playing, and behavioral rehearsal to enhance effective communication of emotions, need for support or information, and disease-related symptoms.

11. Educate patient about the physical mechanism of breathing and possible triggers of asthma attacks (e.g., airborne irritants, allergens, foods, animal dander, dust mites, exercise stress, psychosocial stressors).

12. Ask patient to keep self-monitoring records of asthma attacks, including associated physical symptoms, situational factors preceding attack, and emotions before and during attack.

13. Assist patient in analyzing self-monitoring records to identify potential patterns and asthma triggers.

14. Help patient develop a plan for reducing exposure to those asthma triggers that are avoidable.

15. Educate patient about the effects of stress and anxiety on asthma symptoms and provide rationale for relaxation training.

16. Train patient in relaxation techniques such as diaphragmatic breathing, deep-muscle relaxation, and guided imagery to reduce anticipatory anxiety and autonomic arousal associated with asthma symptoms.

21. Engage in appropriate levels of daily activities (e.g., vocational, recreational, social) and exercise as recommended by physician. (36, 37, 38)

—. _____
   _____

—. _____
   _____

—. _____
   _____

17. Utilize biofeedback training to enhance patient's development of relaxation techniques.

18. Work with patient to develop a hierarchy of feared asthma-related situations and symptoms that contribute to anxiety.

19. Utilize systematic desensitization to reduce anxiety associated with stimuli in the hierarchy.

20. Help patient obtain training in using peak-flow meter to identify onset of asthma exacerbations.

21. Teach patient to utilize deterioration in peak flow (as measured by peak-flow meter) and associated bodily sensations as cues signaling the need to take asthma medication, practice relaxation techniques, or engage in other appropriate self-care activities.

22. Educate family members and/or significant others about asthma. Encourage their support and involvement in patient's adherence to medical treatment regimen and in implementing asthma management strategies.

23. Educate patient and family members about the negative impact of cigarette smoking on asthma symptoms.

24. Assist patient (and family members who smoke) in implementing smoking cessation strategies (see Cigarette Smoking chapter in this *Planner*) or refer for treatment of nicotine addiction.

25. Refer patient for or conduct family therapy to help family members manage stressors and demands associated with patient's medical condition and/or to address family problems that may exacerbate asthma symptoms.

26. Encourage patient and family members to attend an asthma support group. Explore and process impact of attending the group.

27. Explore emotional impact of life changes associated with asthma.

28. Assist patient in identification, awareness, and appropriate expression of emotions associated with medical condition.

29. Assess and treat anxiety, depression, and feelings of helplessness or hopelessness associated with medical condition (see Anxiety and Depression chapters in this *Planner*).

30. Assist patient in identifying internal and external sources of daily stress.

31. Help patient identify life circumstances (e.g., interpersonal, vocational, financial) that can be altered to reduce stress.

32. Encourage and reinforce implementation of changes in life circumstances that will reduce stress.

33. Help patient identify negative, distorted cognitions and irrational beliefs about asthma symptoms and prognosis that contribute to internal stress.

34. Teach patient to replace negative, irrational thoughts with more realistic self-talk.

35. Encourage realistic outlook about symptoms and prognosis while identifying and challenging negative cognitive biases (e.g., catastrophizing, overgeneralization, all-or-none thinking).

36. Address problematic beliefs that contribute to sick role behavior and interfere with normal functioning in terms of work or school responsibilities, exercise, recreation, or social interaction.

37. Encourage and reinforce exercise regimen as medically appropriate.

38. Reinforce patient's involvement in social and recreational activities.

___.   _____
       _____
___.   _____
       _____
___.   _____
       _____

DIAGNOSTIC SUGGESTIONS

Axis I: 316   Psychological Factors Affecting Asthma
               309.24   Adjustment Disorder with Anxiety
               309.28   Adjustment Disorder with Mixed Anxiety and
                           Depressed Mood
               293.89   Anxiety Disorder Due to Asthma
               V15.81   Noncompliance with Treatment
               _____   _____
               _____   _____

CANCER

BEHAVIORAL DEFINITIONS

1. Feelings of depression or anxiety due to diagnosis of cancer.
2. Emotional distress associated with decline in physical health and daily functioning caused by cancer or its treatment.
3. Unresolved grief, anger, fear, or hopelessness associated with diagnosis of terminal illness.
4. Avoidance of talking on anything more than a superficial level about cancer diagnosis.
5. Poorly controlled cancer-related pain that interferes with daily activities and restricts quality of life.
6. Physical symptoms (e.g., nausea and vomiting) or emotional distress associated with medical or surgical treatment for cancer.
7. Cancer treatment ineffectiveness or side effects that lead to lack of compliance with recommended medication regimen or medical procedures (e.g., chemotherapy, radiation therapy, surgery).
8. Continued unhealthy behaviors (e.g., smoking, poor diet, frequent sun exposure) despite a diagnosis of cancer and physician's recommendation to alter these behaviors.

—. _____
   _____
—. _____
   _____
—. _____
   _____

LONG-TERM GOALS

1. Decrease feelings of depression, fear, or anxiety.
2. Improve ability to identify, cope with, and appropriately express emotions associated with cancer diagnosis.
3. Improve quality of life and reduce disruption in daily activities caused by cancer pain and/or decline in physical health.
4. Become as knowledgeable as possible about cancer and available treatment options.
5. Develop attitudes and behaviors that promote feelings of peace, confidence, and acceptance in coping with cancer and corresponding life changes.
6. Increase compliance with and adjustment to necessary medical procedures.
7. Reduce cancer pain by appropriate use of pain-coping strategies and analgesic medication, while minimizing medication side effects.
8. Acquire stress- and pain-management skills to enhance emotional adaptation to disease.
9. Decrease or eliminate behaviors detrimental to health (e.g., cigarette smoking, excessive sun exposure, alcohol abuse, poor diet, high stress) while implementing positive health behaviors (e.g., breast self-examination, low stress, sobriety, balanced diet, exercise, sufficient rest).

—. _____

_____

—. _____

_____

—. _____

_____

SHORT-TERM OBJECTIVES	THERAPEUTIC INTERVENTIONS
1. Describe medical condition, treatment regimen, and prognosis as much as they are understood. (1)	1. Explore patient's understanding of diagnosis, treatment options, and prognosis, while also assessing level of denial.
2. Read information about cancer and verbalize increased knowledge about	2. Assist patient in obtaining verbal and written informa-

medical condition and treatment options. (2, 3, 4)

3. Decrease level of verbal denial regarding cancer diagnosis, treatment options, and prognosis, while increasing verbal acceptance. (5, 6, 7, 17, 25)

4. Verbally express fears about possible deterioration of physical condition and death. (6, 7)

5. Verbalize feelings of grief and loss associated with medical condition. (6, 7, 8)

6. Identify and verbally express feelings of depression or anxiety associated with medical condition. (9, 10, 11, 25)

7. Identify and appropriately express negative emotions in verbal communications with therapist and significant others. (7, 12, 25)

8. Read books regarding cancer-coping strategies and verbalize increased confidence in coping skills. (13)

9. Implement assertiveness to gain knowledge and a sense of control, and to facilitate communication of feelings, questions, symptoms, or needs to family and medical personnel. (14, 15, 20)

10. Comply with medication regimen and necessary medical procedures, reporting any side effects or problems to physicians or therapists. (3, 16, 17)

tion about cancer from sources such as physicians, nurses, the American Cancer Society, and/or reputable Internet sites.

3. Consult with patient's physician and other pertinent medical personnel to enhance coordination of medical and psychological treatments.

4. Assist patient in acquiring information about recommended medical and surgical treatment procedures from physicians, nurses, the American Cancer Society, and/or reputable Internet sites.

5. Gently confront denial of the seriousness of condition and of the need for compliance with medical treatment procedures.

6. Explore and process fears associated with deterioration of physical health, death, and dying.

7. Normalize patient's feelings of grief, sadness, or anxiety associated with medical condition and encourage verbal expression of these emotions.

8. Process feelings of grief associated with changes in health and lifestyle.

9. Explore the emotional impact of life changes associated with cancer.

11. Report to physicians or therapists any physical symptoms (e.g., pain, nausea, growths) that cause concern. (15, 18, 19)

12. Implement distraction and relaxation techniques (i.e., deep-muscle relaxation, imagery, or autogenics) to manage symptoms associated with cancer (e.g., pain) or its treatment (e.g., nausea due to chemotherapy). (21, 22, 23, 24)

13. Create a hierarchy of anxiety-producing procedures and cooperate with systematic desensitization procedures to help manage nausea and vomiting. (23, 24)

14. Attend a cancer support group. (25)

15. Verbalize life circumstances that lead to worry, tension, or stress. (26)

16. Identify circumstances that can be altered to reduce stress and dissatisfaction. (26, 27, 28)

17. Implement changes in life situation (e.g., vocational, financial, legal, social, marital, recreational) to reduce level of stress. (29)

18. Identify and implement strategies to increase sense of control and confidence in coping with daily stressors. (13, 23, 30)

10. Identify and treat depression and anxiety. (See Depression and Anxiety chapters in this *Planner.*)

11. Assign patient to keep a daily journal of emotions, to be shared in therapy sessions.

12. Assist patient in identification, awareness, and appropriate expression of emotions.

13. Recommend books about coping with cancer (e.g., *Helping Yourself: A Workbook for People Living with Cancer* by Cunningham, *Beyond Miracles: Living with Cancer* by Hersch, or *Chicken Soup for the Surviving Soul* by Canfield, Hansen, Aubery, and Mitchell). Process patient's thoughts and emotions about reading the material.

14. Use modeling, role playing, and behavioral rehearsal to teach assertiveness skills (or refer for assertiveness training) to enhance effective communication of emotions, and/or need for support or information.

15. Encourage and reinforce patient's assertiveness in asking questions, expressing needs, describing symptoms, and sharing feelings.

16. Monitor and reinforce patient's compliance with medical treatment regimen.

19. Identify those life circumstances that cannot be changed but must be coped with more effectively. (26, 27, 31)

20. Identify distorted cognitions in response to daily events and illness-related stressors that contribute to anxiety or depression. (32)

21. Replace negative self-talk with more realistic, positive messages that reduce negative affect and promote a positive outlook. (33, 34, 35)

22. Make a commitment to maintain a fighting spirit determined to overcome the physical, spiritual, and psychological threats of cancer. (36)

23. Report on instances of using laughter to reduce tension and anxiety. (36, 37, 38)

24. List whatever blocks the experience of joy and develop a plan to overcome the roadblocks. (38, 39)

25. Identify life priorities and develop a specific plan for implementing those priorities. (40)

26. Identify and utilize sources of social and spiritual support to enhance coping with daily stressors. (25, 41, 42)

27. Terminate the use or abuse of alcohol and/or nicotine. (43, 44)

17. Explore and address misconceptions, fears, and situational factors that interfere with compliance with medical treatment.

18. Assist patient in monitoring physical symptoms that require medical attention and review the necessary steps to obtain appropriate medical care.

19. Assess for presence of cancer pain, including intensity of pain, quality of pain, and aggravating and relieving factors.

20. Help patient to implement strategies that enhance a sense of control in managing medical condition (e.g., increasing assertive communication with medical personnel, taking an active role in treatment plan).

21. Teach patient coping strategies (e.g., distraction and relaxation techniques) to utilize during aversive medical procedures.

22. Teach patient strategies for managing pain exacerbations. (See chapters on Chronic and Acute Pain in this *Planner.*)

23. Train patient in the use of relaxation techniques (e.g., deep-muscle relaxation, positive imagery, and diaphragmatic breathing) to manage symptoms such as nausea or pain.

28. Implement recommended dietary changes, including decreased intake of fat and salt, and increased intake of healthy foods. (45)

29. Maintain a pattern of medically appropriate exercise and a patterned sleep/wake cycle. (46)

30. Comply with lifestyle changes and health behaviors recommended by physician (e.g., decreased sun exposure, regular breast self-examination). (47)

31. Verbalize an attitude of hope, peace, and joy that fights disease. (13, 30, 36, 39, 48)

___. _____

_____

___. _____

_____

___. _____

_____

24. Utilize systematic desensitization to reduce nausea, vomiting, and loss of appetite associated with chemotherapy.

25. Refer patient to a cancer support group and process impact of attending the group.

26. Assist patient in identifying sources of daily stress.

27. Help patient differentiate between stressors that can be altered versus stressors that must be accepted and coped with more effectively.

28. Assist patient in identifying those life circumstances (e.g., interpersonal, financial, or vocational) that can be changed to reduce stress.

29. Encourage and reinforce ongoing implementation of life changes that will reduce stress.

30. Teach patient to use visualization techniques to create positive images of adaptively coping with chronic illness, thereby promoting an optimistic outlook and increasing level of confidence.

31. Assist patient in developing an attitude of acceptance for those things that he/she cannot change.

32. Teach patient to identify negative, distorted cognitions in response to daily hassles and illness-related stressors.

33. Teach patient to replace negative, distorted thoughts with more positive, realistic self-talk.

34. Encourage patient to maintain a realistic outlook regarding prognosis, while identifying and modifying negative cognitive biases (e.g., catastrophizing, overgeneralization).

35. Encourage patient to focus on his/her successes and accomplishments rather than ruminating about what remains undone.

36. Challenge the patient to keep a positive, jovial attitude, as much free from anxiety as possible, thereby creating a biochemical, emotional, and spiritual atmosphere to fight disease and infirmity with healing powers. Recommend reading *You Can Fight for Your Life* (LeShan), *Anatomy of an Illness as Perceived by the Patient: Reflections on Healing and Regeneration* (Cousins and Dubos), and/or *Head First: The Biology of Hope and the Healing Power of the Human Spirit* (Cousins).

37. Assign patient to read a book of humor or jokes and to report on its effects on attitude and/or mood.

38. Assign patient to consciously pursue and experience levity (e.g., watch a humorous movie, keep a log of funny incidents that were

observed in life, record instances of making others laugh).

39. Assign patient to list whatever blocks the experience of joy and discuss a plan to overcome those hindrances.

40. Assign patient to make a list of unfinished tasks and life priorities. Assist patient in developing a plan for completing important tasks and priorities.

41. Ask patient to identify existing sources of social support.

42. Encourage family involvement and support in treatment planning, medical procedures, and implementation of lifestyle changes.

43. Assist patient in implementing smoking cessation strategies (see Cigarette Smoking chapter in this *Planner*) or refer for treatment of nicotine addiction.

44. Assess for the presence of chemical dependence and, if necessary, refer for substance abuse treatment to address chemical dependency.

45. Educate patient regarding proper nutrition to reduce health risks, or refer to a dietician.

46. Encourage patient to establish an exercise regimen as medically appropriate and also a regular sleep/wake cycle.

47. Monitor and reinforce patient's compliance with recommended lifestyle and health behavior changes (e.g., avoiding sun exposure, regular breast self-examination, keeping appointments with doctor).

48. Challenge patient to adopt a perspective of acceptance, dignity, and peace instead of giving in to fear, bitterness, hopelessness, or withdrawal in response to changes in physical health.

___. _____
    _____

___. _____
    _____

___. _____
    _____

DIAGNOSTIC SUGGESTIONS

Axis I: 316   Psychological Factors Affecting Cancer
            307.89   Pain Disorder Associated with Both
                        Psychological Factors and Cancer
            309.0   Adjustment Disorder with Depressed Mood
            309.24   Adjustment Disorder with Anxiety
            309.28   Adjustment Disorder with Mixed Anxiety and
                        Depressed Mood
            V15.81   Noncompliance with Treatment
            _____   _____
            _____   _____

CARDIOVASCULAR DISEASE

BEHAVIORAL DEFINITIONS

1. Occurrence of angina or myocardial infarction due to coronary heart disease.
2. Feelings of anxiety or depression associated with a diagnosed cardiovascular condition.
3. Fear about cardiac symptoms that interferes with daily activities and restricts quality of life.
4. Worry about cardiac condition that causes hesitancy about planning future activities.
5. Continued high-risk behaviors (e.g., smoking, physical inactivity, poor diet) despite diagnosis of cardiovascular disease and physician's recommendation to alter these behaviors.
6. Psychological or behavioral factors that exacerbate cardiac symptoms or influence the course of the cardiovascular condition.
7. Coronary artery bypass graft (CABG) surgery for heart disease.
8. A high level of risk for coronary heart disease (CHD), as indicated by the presence of several risk factors (e.g., hypertension, hypercholesterolemia, obesity, cigarette smoking, physical inactivity, diabetes, and/or family history of CHD).

—. _____

_____

—. _____

_____

—. _____

_____

LONG-TERM GOALS

1. Decrease feelings of depression and anxiety associated with cardiac condition.
2. Improve quality of life and decrease disruption in daily activities caused by cardiac condition.
3. Increase knowledge about cardiovascular disease and the role of behavioral risk factors, while implementing lifestyle changes to improve health status.
4. Identify and change psychological or behavioral factors that contribute to cardiovascular problems.
5. Alter lifestyle factors to reduce risk for occurrence or recurrence of myocardial infarction.
6. Reduce risk for coronary heart disease by altering negative health behaviors and implementing positive health changes.
7. Increase compliance with and adjustment to necessary diagnostic and surgical procedures for cardiac condition.

—. _____

_____

—. _____

_____

—. _____

_____

SHORT-TERM OBJECTIVES

1. Cooperate with a complete physical exam and develop a plan for follow-up medical care. (1, 2)

2. Comply with medical treatment regimen and necessary diagnostic procedures. Take medications as prescribed and report any side effects or problems to physicians or therapists. (1, 2, 3, 4)

THERAPEUTIC INTERVENTIONS

1. Refer patient to physician for a complete physical if not already under the care of a physician.

2. Consult with physician to enhance coordination of medical and behavioral treatments for patient's cardiovascular condition.

3. Monitor and reinforce patient's compliance with medical treatment regimen. Explore and address misin-

3. Increase assertiveness in dealing with medical personnel to gain information and a sense of control. (5)

4. Increase knowledge about cardiovascular disorder. (1, 2, 6)

5. Verbalize an understanding of how lifestyle factors such as diet, exercise, obesity, and smoking can impact heart condition. (6, 7, 8)

6. Identify cognitive, affective, and behavioral changes needed to reduce coronary risk level and improve health. (8, 9, 10)

7. Implement changes in diet, including decreased intake of salt, fat, cholesterol, and excessive calories. (11, 12)

8. Increase regular exercise and daily physical activity as directed by physician. (13, 17, 18)

9. Implement a plan for stopping smoking. (14)

10. Identify feelings of depression, anxiety, or fear associated with medical condition. (15, 16, 17)

11. Verbalize fears associated with return to normal functioning in social, recreational, vocational, and sexual arenas following cardiac rehabilitation. (17, 18)

12. List circumstances in life that lead to worry, tension, unhappiness, or stress. (19)

formation, beliefs, fears, and situational factors that contribute to lack of compliance with treatment regimen.

4. Educate patient about the role of recommended medical diagnostic procedures (such as cardiac catheterization). Explore fears and concerns regarding these procedures. Teach patient coping strategies (e.g., distraction and relaxation techniques) to utilize during aversive procedures.

5. Work with patient to implement strategies that enhance a sense of control and self-efficacy in managing medical condition (e.g., assertiveness training to improve interactions with medical personnel, increasing knowledge about medical condition, taking an active role in treatment plan).

6. Provide patient with literature that explains heart disease, its causes, treatment, and impact on quality of life.

7. Explain the role of psychological interventions in reducing coronary risk factors and enhancing the ability to cope with life changes.

8. Educate patient about lifestyle risk factors for coronary heart disease (e.g., cigarette smoking, high cholesterol, hypertension, obesity).

13. Identify those life circumstances that can be altered to reduce stress and dissatisfaction. (20, 21)

14. Implement changes in life situation (vocational, social, familial, marital, financial, recreational) that lead to reduced stress. (22, 23)

15. Identify those life circumstances that cannot be changed but that must be coped with more effectively. (24)

16. Practice relaxation techniques (e.g., deep-muscle relaxation) on a daily basis to relieve tension and cope with daily stressors. (25, 26)

17. Identify and implement strategies to enhance sense of control in coping with daily stressors. (27)

18. Identify distorted cognitive self-talk that precipitates anxiety or depression in response to environmental events. (28)

19. Replace negative self-talk with more realistic, positive messages that reduce anxiety and lift spirits. (29)

20. Increase awareness of Type A behaviors (e.g., impatience, verbal and behavioral hostility, competitiveness) and how these may negatively impact cardiovascular condition. (30, 31)

9. Educate patient about the interplay of cognitive, behavioral, emotional, and physiological responses, and their impact on cardiovascular functioning.

10. Review risk factors and identify those that are most problematic for patient.

11. Provide education about proper nutrition and eating habits to decrease blood cholesterol level and to normalize weight. (See chapter on Obesity in this *Planner*.)

12. Refer patient to nutritionist or dietician for nutritional counseling and weight management.

13. Educate patient about the importance of exercise in reducing cardiovascular risk. Monitor compliance with exercise regimen recommended by physician.

14. Assist patient in implementing smoking cessation strategies. (See Cigarette Smoking chapter in this *Planner*.)

15. Explore the emotional impact of life changes associated with cardiac condition.

16. Identify and treat coexisting depression or anxiety. (See Depression and Anxiety chapters in this *Planner*.)

17. Explore and address fears and concerns that interfere with patient resuming medically recommended levels of activity following myocar-

21. Decrease Type A behaviors as evidenced by decreased impatience, hostile behaviors, and competitiveness. (31, 32)

22. Verbally acknowledge and express feelings of grief and loss associated with changes in health status. (15, 33, 34)

23. Identify and utilize sources of social support in making lifestyle changes and enhancing adjustment to heart disease. (35, 36, 37)

24. Attend a heart disease recovery support group. (35, 37)

25. Gradually resume regular daily activities after myocardial infarction or cardiac surgery, following doctor's orders regarding any activity limitations and reporting any physical symptoms that cause concern. (11, 13, 17, 18, 38)

—. _____
   _____

—. _____
   _____

—. _____
   _____

dial infarction or cardiac surgery.

18. Address problematic beliefs that contribute to prolonged sick role behavior and that interfere with return to normal functioning in terms of exercise, work responsibilities, recreation, sexual behavior, and social interaction.

19. Assist patient in identifying all sources of stress in his/her life.

20. Help patient differentiate between those stressors that can be altered versus those that must be accepted and coped with.

21. Help patient identify those vocational, social, interpersonal, financial, or recreational circumstances in life that can be changed to reduce stress.

22. Develop an action plan to take control of those circumstances that can be altered to reduce stress.

23. Encourage and reinforce ongoing implementation of life changes that will reduce stress.

24. Assist patient in identifying those sources of stress that require acceptance and more effective coping skills.

25. Train patient in the use of relaxation techniques such as deep-muscle relaxation, guided imagery, and diaphragmatic breathing.

26. Administer biofeedback to help patient apply relaxation strategies to reduce blood pressure, muscle tension, and overall physiological reactivity.

27. Help patient to develop problem-solving, time-management, and/or communication skills to enhance coping with daily stressors.

28. Teach patient to identify negative, distorted cognitions in response to stressors.

29. Teach patient to replace distorted, negative thoughts with more positive, realistic self-talk.

30. Assess for the presence of Type A behaviors. If patient exhibits these behaviors, educate about research linking Type A behavior to increased risk for cardiac problems.

31. Confront patient actions and statements that reflect Type A behaviors (e.g., lack of concern for others, extreme impatience, hostile behaviors). Explore patient's attitudes and beliefs that maintain Type A behavior.

32. Implement strategies to address Type A behaviors. (See Type A Behavior chapter in *The Complete Adult Psychotherapy Treatment Planner*.)

33. Assist patient in processing feelings of grief related to changes in health and lifestyle.

34. Challenge patient to a perspective of acceptance and peace rather than fear, bitterness, and withdrawal as a response to changes in health and lifestyle.

35. Ask patient to identify existing sources of social support. Discuss ways to utilize support system to prompt and reinforce positive changes in health behaviors.

36. Encourage family involvement and support in treatment planning and implementation of lifestyle changes.

37. Refer patient to a heart disease support group. Process impact of attending group with therapist.

38. Monitor patient for physical symptoms that may require immediate medical attention and process the necessary steps to obtain appropriate medical care.

__. _____
_____

__. _____
_____

__. _____
_____

DIAGNOSTIC SUGGESTIONS

Axis I: 316   Psychological Factors Affecting Cardiovascular
                      Disease
             309.0   Adjustment Disorder with Depressed Mood
             309.24   Adjustment Disorder with Anxiety
             309.28   Adjustment Disorder with Mixed Anxiety and
                      Depressed Mood
             V15.81   Noncompliance with Treatment
             293.89   Anxiety Disorder Due to Cardiovascular
                      Disease
             305.10   Nicotine Dependence

             _____   _____

             _____   _____

CHRONIC FATIGUE SYNDROME (CFS)

BEHAVIORAL DEFINITIONS

1. Relentless fatigue not substantially alleviated by rest and not the result of ongoing exertion or other diagnosable medical condition.
2. Concurrent occurrence of relatively minor symptoms such as sore throat, muscle pain, weakness, low-grade fever, impairment in concentration, etc.
3. Substantial reduction in occupational, social, and recreational activities for at least six months.
4. Experience of "burnout" even though previously very active, compulsive, overextended.
5. Difficulty in sleeping, or excessive sleep that remains unrefreshing ("nonrestorative").
6. Moderate exercise is extremely difficult and strenuous exercise is avoided.
7. Mild to severe depression and anxiety coupled with feelings of being misunderstood and stigmatized.
8. Poor communication and high frustration level with health professionals, who may not take condition seriously.
9. Irritability leading to strained relationships with family, friends, and employers.

__. _____
_____
_____

__. _____
_____
_____

__. _____
_____

LONG-TERM GOALS

1. Reduce feelings of helplessness while increasing feelings of successfully coping with fatigue.
2. Become as knowledgeable and self-reliant as possible in coping with CFS.
3. Increase activity level and decrease time spent in bed or on couch.
4. Learn and practice ways of thinking that help avoid a preoccupation with symptoms.
5. Strive to maintain as normal a life as possible, rather than waiting for a cure.
6. Reduce fatigue and emotional suffering.
7. Establish a relationship with a physician who is supportive and knowledgeable about CFS but does not overtreat the condition.
8. Accept the fact that there is no specific treatment that has proven to be effective for CFS.
9. Develop effective psychophysiologic self-regulating skills.

—. _____

_____

—. _____

_____

—. _____

_____

SHORT-TERM OBJECTIVES

1. Describe the history, medical management, and present manifestations of CFS. (1, 4)

2. Identify the negative effects CFS has had on life. (2)

3. Verbalize an understanding of the key concepts regarding management of CFS. (3, 4)

THERAPEUTIC INTERVENTIONS

1. Assess the patient's fatigue problem: its onset, severity, perceived cause(s), treatment, management.

2. Explore how the patient's life has changed since the onset of CFS.

3. Review patient's past medical records. Ensure that other physical illnesses have been ruled out with a reasonable degree of confidence.

4. Establish a trusting relationship with an understanding physician, even if little can be done to treat CFS. (4)

5. Acquire information and verbalize an understanding of the known facts about CFS. (5, 6)

6. Verbalize acceptance of the fact that CFS is poorly understood and difficult to treat by medical science. (5, 6, 7)

7. Verbalize understanding and acceptance of the fact that successful CFS management depends largely on attitude and behaviors. (8, 9)

8. Verbalize satisfaction with reasonable improvement in activity level, mood, and energy, rather than expecting disappearance of all symptoms. (10)

9. Follow a plan for gradually increasing daily activity level. (11, 12, 13)

10. Accurately self-monitor and report fatigue, mood, activity level, sleep, and medication use. (14)

11. Plan and follow a daily schedule that allows for proper pacing of activity level. (13, 15, 16)

12. Verbalize any personal or family history of depression that predates the onset of CFS. (17, 18)

4. Explore patient's current medical management plan; if indicated, refer to doctor who is interested and knowledgeable about CFS.

5. Assist the patient in obtaining written information about causes and management of CFS. Contact Chronic Fatigue and Immune Dysfunction Syndrome Association of America at Internet site: www.cfids.org.

6. Discuss with the patient the fact that medical treatment consists primarily of trial-and-error use of drugs such as antivirals, antidepressants, anti-inflammatories, and immunomodulators.

7. Provide information, encouragement, and support to combat patient's feelings of being misunderstood and overwhelmed.

8. Sympathize with patient's struggle with fatigue and feelings of being misunderstood, but challenge passivity.

9. Challenge patient's putting life on "hold" while waiting for remedy for fatigue. Instead, encourage talk about necessary adjustments to prior daily activities.

10. Encourage talk about feasible short-term behavioral goals in place of vague, overly comprehensive statements like wanting to have "more energy."

13. Verbalize any history or present incidence of suicidal ideation. (18)

14. Assertively ask clear questions of those people involved in treatment. (19, 20)

15. Report any improvements in sleep pattern after implementing behavioral sleep techniques. (21, 27)

16. Increase the amount of daily physical exercise as a means of building physical strength, reducing stress, and improving mood. (22, 23, 27)

17. Change to diet that is balanced in the five major food groups and eat meals on a regular daily schedule. (24, 25, 26, 27)

18. Verbalize an understanding of the link between emotional/attitudinal state and physical symptoms. (28, 29, 30)

19. Verbalize an understanding that inactivity, boredom, and a lack of making a contribution to life can lead to depression. (29, 30)

20. Verbalize feelings of depression and anxiety that may contribute to fatigue. (31)

21. Identify automatic thoughts that can trigger negative emotional responses. (32, 33)

22. Increase use of positive self-talk in response to fatigue. (34)

11. Help the patient establish a behavioral plan for a gradual increase in daily activity level, and reinforce increases as they are reported.

12. Urge the patient to avoid resorting to complete bed rest, which will only result in progressive muscle deconditioning.

13. Aid the patient in finding an appropriate ceiling for current daily activities. Have patient budget energy by working to tolerance, then resting before resuming activity (rather than exerting beyond limits).

14. Teach the patient to maintain self-monitoring log and to use it to spot changes and connections between fatigue, mood, activity level, medication use, sleep, etc.

15. Review daily activity log to reinforce proper pacing of activity versus overexertion or inactivity.

16. Teach patient how to say no; encourage setting limits on accepting social obligations and commitments.

17. Carefully explore the degree to which the patient's fatigue is of pure CFS type or comorbid with psychiatric symptoms.

18. Evaluate level of depression, support system, and suicide potential; take appropriate safety precautions for patient if necessary.

23. Verbalize ways to reduce frustration and manage anger toward those who seem critical and unsupportive. (35, 42, 43)

24. Learn and use psychophysiologic self-relaxation skills (i.e., slow/deep breathing, muscle relaxation, hand warming) to aid in management of pain and stress. (36, 37, 38)

25. Reduce the level of reactivity to environmental stress. (34, 37, 39)

26. Verbalize an understanding that bed rest and inactivity are seldom helpful for this condition and report the benefits of increased activity on feelings of well-being, improved mood, and increased self-esteem. (40)

27. Make use of personal, vocational, and marital/family counseling as needed. (41)

__. _____
   _____

__. _____
   _____

__. _____
   _____

19. Teach the patient assertiveness skills or refer to an assertiveness training class.

20. Use role playing and behavioral rehearsal to teach the patient to be assertive in asking clear questions of medical personnel.

21. Encourage the patient to use behavioral sleep techniques (e.g., retire at the same time each night, utilize relaxation skills, take warm bath before bed, avoid spices or caffeine in diet).

22. Assist the patient in developing a daily routine of physical exercise.

23. Recommend that the patient read and implement programs from *Exercising Your Way to Better Mental Health* by Leith.

24. Assist the patient in planning meals that are balanced to give adequate nutrition and improve health and energy.

25. Refer the patient to a dietician for meal planning and dietary education.

26. Urge the patient to eat meals on a regular schedule to promote routine in eating, sleeping, and activity.

27. Monitor patient's diet, times of eating, exercise, and sleep cycle, refocusing behavior as necessary.

28. Raise the patient's awareness of mind/body relationships.

29. Aid the patient in separating physical discomfort from emotional suffering.

30. Encourage the patient to consider the links between inactivity and depression.

31. Help the patient to recognize and modify emotional response patterns and behaviors (e.g., unresolved grief, cue-generated panic, anger over past abuse) that may be rooted in past experiences and are being reactivated and magnified by CFS symptoms.

32. Teach the patient how negative cognitive distortions can readily lead to feelings of helplessness and anger.

33. Assist the patient in identifying distorted cognitive self-talk that fosters depression or anxiety.

34. Teach and reinforce positive, realistic cognitive self-talk as a means of coping with fatigue and depression.

35. Instruct patient in anger-management skills (e.g., practicing forgiveness and tolerance, being assertive versus aggressive, delayed responding).

36. Instruct the patient in developing psychophysiological self-regulation skills through use of such cognitive techniques as focused attention and visualization.

37. Instruct patient in relaxation skills (e.g., use of breath control, systematic deep-muscle relaxation, hand/foot warming).

38. Provide the patient with cassette tapes and written material for home practice of self-regulation skills.

39. Assist the patient in recognizing sources of environmental stress and in developing a plan for reducing those that can be changed.

40. Reinforce the patient's reports of activity rather than allowing inactivity as the primary coping mechanism for pain, low energy, and depression.

41. Recommend personal, family, or couple counseling if relationships are significantly strained by CFS.

42. Promote acceptance of responsibility, while helping the patient deal with feelings of guilt stemming from inability to meet perceived obligations.

43. Teach the patient how a need to "prove" the legitimacy of one's symptoms can become a hindrance to the coping process.

___.   _____
       _____
___.   _____
       _____
___.   _____
       _____

DIAGNOSTIC SUGGESTIONS

Axis I: 310.1   Personality Change Due to Chronic Fatigue
Syndrome
296.xx   Major Depressive Disorder
300.4   Dysthymic Disorder
307.80   Pain Disorder Associated with Psychological
Factors
300.81   Somatization Disorder
300.81   Undifferentiated Somatoform Disorder
780.59   Sleep Disorder, Mixed Type

_____   _____
_____   _____

CHRONIC OBSTRUCTIVE PULMONARY DISEASE (COPD)

BEHAVIORAL DEFINITIONS

1. Airflow obstruction due to chronic bronchitis or emphysema.
2. Symptoms of dyspnea, coughing, wheezing, sputum production, impaired gas exchange, and frequent respiratory infections.
3. Feelings of anxiety associated with COPD symptoms or anticipation of COPD symptoms.
4. Symptoms of COPD interfere with daily activities and restrict quality of life.
5. Worry about future episodes of dyspnea that causes hesitancy in planning or initiating activities.
6. Feelings of depression, helplessness, or hopelessness associated with COPD.
7. Continued use of nicotine despite diagnosis of COPD and physician's recommendation to quit smoking.
8. Lack of compliance with medical treatment regimen.

—. _____

_____

—. _____

_____

—. _____

_____

LONG-TERM GOALS

1. Increase knowledge about COPD and medical treatment options.
2. Slow progression of the disease and minimize severity of physical symptoms.
3. Increase sense of self-efficacy in managing COPD symptoms.

4. Reduce fear, anxiety, and worry associated with COPD.
5. Decrease feelings of depression or hopelessness.
6. Improve quality of life and reduce disruption in daily activities caused by COPD.
7. Acquire stress-management skills to enhance emotional adaptation to chronic disease.
8. Eliminate cigarette smoking.
9. Achieve and maintain compliance with medical treatment regimen.

—. _____

_____

—. _____

_____

—. _____

_____

SHORT-TERM OBJECTIVES

1. Describe medical condition, treatment regimen, and prognosis to therapist. (1)

2. Verbalize increased knowledge about COPD. (2, 3)

3. Comply with medical treatment regimen, reporting any problems or side effects to appropriate medical personnel. (4, 5, 6, 7)

4. Report physical symptoms that cause concern to physician or therapist using assertive communication skills. (7, 8)

5. Increase assertiveness with health care professionals to gain a greater sense of control in managing COPD. (8, 9)

THERAPEUTIC INTERVENTIONS

1. Explore patient's understanding of his/her lung disease, prognosis, current treatment regimen, and treatment options.

2. Assist patient in obtaining information about COPD from physicians, the American Lung Association, and/or reputable Internet sites.

3. Consult with patient's physician and other pertinent medical personnel to clarify treatment regimen, physical limitations, and prognosis, and to enhance coordination of medical and behavioral treatment.

4. Monitor and reinforce patient's compliance with medical treatment regimen, including prescribed in-

6. Verbalize increased knowledge about factors that may exacerbate COPD symptoms. (10, 12, 18)

7. Make changes in environment or in daily routine to reduce exposure to irritants that exacerbate symptoms. (10, 11)

8. Develop and implement a plan for smoking cessation that involves all smokers in the household. (12, 13, 14)

9. Implement healthy dietary changes as recommended by nutritionist to maintain adequate levels of nutrition. (15)

10. Attend a support group for individuals with COPD and process emotional reactions with therapist. (16)

11. Maintain a pattern of medically appropriate exercise as recommended by physician or pulmonary rehabilitation specialist. (17, 44)

12. Practice relaxation techniques regularly to reduce tension and to cope with daily stressors. (18, 19, 20, 21)

13. Utilize slow, deep breathing with pursed-lip exhalation to manage episodes of dyspnea. (20)

14. Cooperate with systematic desensitization procedures to reduce anxiety associated with COPD symptoms. (22, 23)

halers, medications, ventilator, and bronchial hygiene techniques; use behavioral contracting to increase compliance as needed.

5. Explore and address patient's fears, inaccurate beliefs, cognitive impairment, and situational factors that interfere with medical treatment compliance.

6. Help patient develop strategies to enhance adherence to medical treatment regimen, such as self-monitoring of medication use through record keeping or use of medication organizer and accepting prompts from family members.

7. Assist patient in identifying physical symptoms that require immediate medical attention; review steps to obtain prompt medical care.

8. Encourage and reinforce patient's assertiveness in seeking information and expressing disease-related concerns and symptoms to medical personnel.

9. Use modelling and role playing to teach assertive communication.

10. Educate patient about environmental irritants that may exacerbate COPD symptoms (e.g., smoke, fumes, dust).

11. Help patient develop a plan for reducing exposure to respiratory system irritants.

15. Develop an action plan of coping strategies to utilize during exacerbations of COPD symptoms. (4, 19, 20, 24)

16. List life circumstances that contribute to stress, worry, or dissatisfaction, and identify those that can be altered to decrease stress level. (25)

17. Identify and utilize support system to assist in implementing COPD management strategies and to enhance ability to cope with disease-related stressors. (26, 27, 33)

18. Attend family therapy session to verbalize need for the support of family members. (28, 30, 31, 32, 33)

19. Report any observed changes in memory, concentration, or thinking to therapist. (29)

20. Verbalize a plan for coping with changes in cognitive functioning and for managing future deterioration in physical health. (28, 30, 31, 32)

21. Implement strategies for improving communication and quality of relationships with significant others. (33)

22. Appropriately express needs, concerns, and feelings in verbal communications with therapist, family, and friends. (9, 33, 34, 36)

12. Educate patient and family members about the role that smoking plays in the development and progression of COPD.

13. Emphasize the importance of smoking cessation in slowing progression of the disease and enhancing the patient's health and quality of life.

14. Assist patient (and household members who smoke) in implementing smoking-cessation procedures (see Cigarette Smoking chapter in this *Planner*) or refer for treatment of nicotine addiction.

15. Refer patient to a dietician or nutritionist to address nutritional deficiencies.

16. Refer patient to a COPD support group and process feelings about the experience.

17. Monitor and reinforce patient's compliance with medically recommended exercise regimen; utilize goal-setting and behavioral contracting to enhance compliance.

18. Educate patient about the effects of stress and anxiety on respiratory symptoms (e.g., hyperventilation, increased dyspnea) and provide rationale for relaxation training.

19. Teach patient relaxation strategies such as deep-muscle relaxation and guided imagery.

23. Identify and verbally express emotions associated with COPD and corresponding changes in daily functioning. (34, 35, 36, 37, 38)

24. Identify life priorities, goals, and aspirations, and develop a specific plan to implement them. (39)

25. Identify negatively distorted, irrational beliefs about medical condition. (40, 41, 42)

26. Replace negative cognitions with more positive, realistic messages. (40, 41, 42, 44)

27. Engage in medically appropriate levels of daily activities (e.g., vocational, leisure, social) as recommended by physician. (43, 44, 45, 46)

28. Identify enjoyable activities and incorporate them into daily life. (45, 46)

—. _____
   _____

—. _____
   _____

—. _____
   _____

20. Train patient in deep, slow diaphragmatic breathing and pursed-lip breathing to help manage dyspnea and associated anxiety.

21. Use biofeedback training to enhance development of relaxation techniques.

22. Help patient construct a hierarchy of disease-related symptoms and circumstances that contribute to anxiety.

23. Implement systematic desensitization procedures to reduce anxiety associated with stimuli in hierarchy.

24. Help patient devise a plan to cope with episodes of shortness of breath, including use of medications, inhalers, relaxation techniques, and/or breathing strategies.

25. Assist patient in identifying internal and external sources of daily stress and in implementing life changes that will reduce stress.

26. Ask patient to list individuals who are sources of social support (e.g., family, friends, neighbors).

27. Encourage involvement of support network in treatment planning, adherence to treatment regimen, and implementation of disease-management strategies.

28. Meet with and educate family members regarding their

need to support compliance with medical management strategies and to assist with obtaining emergency aid if a medical crisis occurs.

29. Monitor deficits in patient's cognitive functioning (e.g., memory, concentration, mental status). If needed refer patient to appropriate health care professionals (e.g., neurologist and/or neuropsychologist) to assess for cognitive decline secondary to hypoxemia.

30. Help patient and family members develop strategies to compensate for patient's cognitive deficits. Strategies include use of lists and calendars, breaking difficult tasks down into smaller steps, bringing family members to doctor's appointments, etc.

31. Assist patient and family members in anticipating and developing an action plan for future declines in physical health (i.e., with respect to finances, treatment decisions, and identifying individuals to assist with caregiving).

32. Encourage patient to discuss with family members desires and preferences regarding end-of-life issues (e.g., decisions about withdrawal of life-sustaining treatment).

33. Conduct or refer patient for marital or family therapy to

address interpersonal conflict, role changes, and other adjustment issues associated with medical condition.

34. Explore emotional impact on patient of lung disease and corresponding life changes.

35. Identify and treat coexisting depression or anxiety. (See Depression and Anxiety chapters in this *Planner.*)

36. Assist patient in identification, awareness, and appropriate expression of emotions associated with medical condition.

37. Explore and process patient's fears associated with deterioration of health, death, and dying.

38. Assist patient in appropriately grieving losses associated with illness (e.g., decline in health and functioning, lifestyle changes, loss of anticipated retirement plans).

39. Assign patient to make a list of life priorities. Assist in developing an action plan for completing important tasks, goals, and priorities.

40. Help patient identify and challenge irrational beliefs about COPD symptoms and prognosis.

41. Encourage patient to develop a realistic outlook regarding symptoms, prognosis, and limitations, while

challenging cognitive distortions and biases (e.g., catastrophizing, all-or-none thinking, overgeneralization).

42. Teach patient cognitive strategies for accurately evaluating disease-related risks, rather than panicking about the possibilities.

43. Assist patient in developing energy conservation strategies, such as simplifying daily activities and utilizing pacing skills.

44. Address irrational fears and faulty beliefs that contribute to prolonged sick role behavior and interfere with medically appropriate levels of functioning in terms of exercise, daily responsibilities, recreation, and social interaction.

45. Assist patient in developing rewarding and enjoyable daily activities to increase life satisfaction.

46. Reinforce patient's involvement in social and recreational activities.

___. _____

_____

___. _____

_____

___. _____

_____

DIAGNOSTIC SUGGESTIONS

Axis I:	316	Psychological Factors Affecting Chronic Obstructive Pulmonary Disease
	309.0	Adjustment Disorder with Depressed Mood
	309.24	Adjustment Disorder with Anxiety
	309.28	Adjustment Disorder with Mixed Anxiety and Depressed Mood
	293.89	Anxiety Disorder Due to Chronic Obstructive Pulmonary Disease
	V15.81	Noncompliance with Treatment
	_____	_____
	_____	_____

CHRONIC PAIN

BEHAVIORAL DEFINITIONS

1. Persistent pain of more than three months' duration.
2. Reduction (or complete loss) in ability to engage in normal daily social, vocational, and recreational activities.
3. Erroneous beliefs about the causes and treatments for pain.
4. Depression and anxiety about pain and associated loss of functional capacity.
5. Overreliance on and preoccupation with pain medication.
6. Troublesome cognitive and behavioral side effects from medication.
7. Excessive, nonproductive changing from one doctor to another.
8. Adversarial relationship with employer, doctors, and/or insurance case managers who are perceived as nonsupportive.
9. Lack of consistent compliance with prescribed treatment or rehabilitation efforts because of pain.
10. Loss of self-esteem due to disability or challenges to disabled status.
11. Irritability leading to strained relationships with family and caretakers.

__. _____
_____

__. _____
_____

__. _____
_____

LONG-TERM GOALS

1. Reduce physical pain and emotional suffering.
2. Become as knowledgeable and self-reliant as possible in coping with chronic pain.
3. Reduce feelings of helplessness while increasing feelings of successfully coping with pain.
4. Improve overall mood and get restful sleep, while coping with and accepting pain.
5. Learn more about causes and regulation of chronic pain.
6. Stop changing physicians, developing sufficient confidence in current pain-management plan.
7. Become an active participant alongside treatment specialists in managing pain.
8. Increase daily activity level and live as full a life as possible within physical limitations.
9. Learn about and follow the prescribed role for medications in managing pain.
10. Develop effective psychophysiologic self-regulation skills.

—. _____

_____

—. _____

_____

—. _____

_____

SHORT-TERM OBJECTIVES

1. Describe type and history of pain symptoms as well as pain-management efforts. (1, 2)
2. Read informative material to increase knowledge of coping with chronic pain. (3)
3. Verbalize an understanding of key concepts regarding management of chronic pain. (3, 4)

THERAPEUTIC INTERVENTIONS

1. Assess patient's pain: its history, severity, type, location, perceived cause(s), treatment, management, effects on life, etc.
2. Discuss the details of patient's pain-management plan. If medical contribution appears inadequate, make a referral to physician or program specializing in pain management.

4. Verbalize accurate information regarding causes for and management of own pain. (3, 4, 5)

5. Verbalize trust in current treating physician. (6)

6. Become an active, self-reliant participant in pain-management plan. (5, 7)

7. Verbalize satisfaction with reasonable progress in controlling mood, activity, and pain, rather than expecting complete pain relief. (8)

8. Eliminate most emergent behavior (e.g., ER visits, using other's medication, calling early for prescription refills). (9)

9. Assertively ask clear questions of people involved in treatment and rehabilitation. (7, 10)

10. Verbalize an understanding of the role that various types of medications play in pain management. (3, 11)

11. Accurately self-monitor and report pain, mood, activity level, and medication. (12)

12. Verbalize an understanding of the rationale and mutual responsibilities of all parties, if physician or pain program requires a signed narcotic contract. (13)

13. Use medication as prescribed and report benefits and problems to therapist and doctors. (11, 14, 15)

14. Cooperate with chemical dependence evaluation. (15)

3. Assist patient in obtaining verbal and written information about causes and management of chronic pain. Recommend reading *Learning to Master Your Chronic Pain* (Jamison), *The Chronic Pain Control Workbook* (Catalano), or *Free Yourself from Pain* (Bresler).

4. Teach patient key concepts in pain management, including rehabilitation versus biologic healing process; conservative versus aggressive medical interventions; differences between acute and chronic pain, between benign and nonbenign pain, and between cure and management; appropriate use of medication; and role of exercise and self-regulation techniques.

5. Assess patient's core beliefs about causes and control of chronic pain. Challenge and help patient correct faulty beliefs (e.g., "It's the doctor's responsibility to cure me," or "I should be better by now").

6. Explore feelings toward treating physician and encourage an attitude of trust.

7. Challenge passivity; reward active patient participation in all aspects of pain management.

8. Encourage talk about feasible short-term behavioral goals in place of vague, overly comprehensive state-

15. Keep primary-care physician informed and allow him or her to monitor all treatments from specialist. (10, 16)

16. Identify the necessary life changes that are dictated by the medical condition. (17)

17. Report on interests and activities that can and will be maintained despite pain, rather than putting life on hold while waiting for pain to go away. (17, 18)

18. Follow recommended physical therapy and exercise program. (7, 19)

19. Plan daily schedule to allow for proper pacing of activity level. (12, 20)

20. Acknowledge frustration and depression over lost functions, while actively seeking to develop feasible alternative interests and activities. (21, 22)

21. Make appropriate use of personal, vocational, and marital/family counseling. (21, 23)

22. Verbalize realistic expectations regarding what family and friends can do to help—do not vent frustration on the innocent. (24)

23. Express needs to others without creating impression of being a whiner or complainer. (24, 25)

ments like wanting to be "pain-free" or "just normal."

9. Enlist patient's cooperation in setting firm limits on emergency treatment of pain, choosing instead to be more planful and systematic about pain management.

10. Discuss with patient what questions to ask and information to give to physicians, employers, insurance representatives, etc., and rehearse with patient how to ask such questions. Teach appropriate assertiveness.

11. Present patient with facts about pain-treatment medications (e.g., discuss differences between narcotic and nonnarcotic analgesics, between steroid and nonsteroidal anti-inflammatories, between psychoactive and nonpsychoactive medications, tranquilizers versus antidepressant, use of antiseizure medications).

12. Teach patient to maintain self-monitoring records and how to use them to spot changes and connections amongst pain, mood, activity level, medication use, and sleep.

13. Explain and have patient sign narcotic contract specifying agreement to use medication only as prescribed (recognizing the risks involved) and to have

24. Verbalize desire to keep adversarial relationships with employer, lawyers, doctors, insurance representatives, etc. from interfering with pain management and rehabilitation progress. (26, 27, 28)

25. Seek out fair and impartial legal advice if that should be necessary. (27, 28)

26. Verbalize adaptive spiritual and philosophic attitudes toward pain and limitations. (18, 29)

27. Cooperate with neuropsychological assessment. (30)

28. Identify and reduce sources of external stress contributing to pain that can reasonably be changed or avoided. (31)

29. Report decrease in fear of being overwhelmed by pain attack. (32)

30. Verbalize feelings of depression and anxiety that may result from or contribute to pain. (21, 32, 33)

31. Identify how pain sensations have opened up negative emotions from past events that were accompanied by similar feelings of being overwhelmed, helpless, and/or fearful. (21, 33)

32. Verbalize a willingness and desire to implement cognitive-behavioral pain-management techniques. (34)

pain medication prescribed by only one physician or pain program.

14. Monitor patient's medication usage as to effectiveness, side effects, and prescription level compliance.

15. Refer for or perform a chemical dependence evaluation, but avoid misconstruing pain-relief-seeking behavior as synonymous with drug-seeking behavior.

16. Encourage open communication between patient and primary-care physician, allowing that physician to monitor all specialists' treatment and medications.

17. Encourage patient to talk about long-term concerns regarding job, financial security, self-esteem, and/or role in family, identifying changes that must be adjusted to.

18. Challenge patient to list interests, activities, and role functions that can be maintained despite the pain.

19. Encourage, monitor, and reinforce patient's follow-through in attending physical therapy and in performing exercise prescribed by physical therapist.

20. Explain to the patient and family the concept of activity pacing as a pain-coping strategy.

33. Identify distorted, self-defeating automatic thoughts that trigger debilitating emotional responses to pain or other sources of stress. (35, 36)

34. Increase use of positive self-talk in response to daily pain or other sources of stress. (36, 37)

35. Utilize cognitive techniques of focused attention and visualization as physiological self-regulation skills. (38)

36. Implement self-relaxation skill involving breath control, muscle relaxation, and mental imagery to manage physical and emotional reactions to pain. (39, 40, 41)

37. Learn and use the cognitive self-analgesia strategies of focusing attention on pleasant, distracting images and sensations to inhibit discomfort. (42)

38. Report instances of improved sleep in a normal sleep/wake cycle. (43)

39. Implement positive health-related behaviors that may reduce pain and increase coping ability. (44)

__. _____
   _____
__. _____
   _____
__. _____
   _____

21. Encourage patient to discuss lost hopes and dreams as a part of the process of grieving over lost abilities. (See Depression chapter in this *Planner*.)

22. Assign patient to list new interests and activities that could be pursued, given the current physical limitations.

23. Recommend personal, family, or couple counseling if relationships are significantly strained by patient's chronic pain condition.

24. Explore ways for patient to avoid focusing interactions with others around pain and disability.

25. Discuss handling of physical aids and physical assistance and how patient should communicate need for assistance to others. Role play and model this communication skill.

26. Discuss how a need to "prove" the legitimacy of one's pain and disability can become a hindrance to the recovery process.

27. Help patient think through the potential utility as well as the pitfalls of legal counsel in dealing with medical, employment, and insurance systems.

28. Explore patient expectations regarding financial compensation for injuries, pain, and disability.

29. Facilitate patient talk about issues such as why pain-causing misfortune happened, justice and fairness, fate and God's purpose.

30. Recognize and intervene where behavioral effects of acute or chronic neuropsychological cognitive impairments may be confused with effects of pain. Perform or refer for neuropsychological assessment if in doubt.

31. Assist patient in recognizing sources of environmental stress and in reducing those that can be changed.

32. Point out the difference between pain as a sensation and pain as emotional suffering.

33. Teach patient ways to recognize and modify emotional response patterns and behaviors that may be rooted in past experiences but that are currently being reactivated and magnified by pain and disability.

34. Aid patient in understanding the integration of a cognitive-behavioral pain-management plan with appropriate medication use.

35. Teach patient how negative, distorted cognitions (e.g., overgeneralization, catastrophizing, all-or-none thinking) can mediate (or exaggerate) a dysfunctional emotional, behavioral,

and/or physiological response to pain and stress.

36. Assist patient in identifying negative automatic thoughts that precipitate depression, tension, and/or exacerbated pain.

37. Teach and reinforce patient's use of positive realistic, cognitive self-talk as a means of coping with pain and depression.

38. Train patient in comprehending and using the cognitive techniques of focused attention and visualization, as tools for psychophysiological self-regulation.

39. Teach patient how to develop and use self-relaxation skills such as breath control, muscle relaxation, positive imagery, and hand/foot warming.

40. Provide patient with cassette tapes for home practice of self-regulation skills.

41. Use biofeedback as an aid in training self-relaxation and self-analgesia.

42. Teach patient how to move from self-relaxation to self-induced analgesia via a deeper application of attentional and visualization skills.

43. Teach patient behavioral sleep techniques (e.g., use relaxation techniques, eliminate naps, establish a presleep ritual).

44. Help patient to identify and
    implement patterned
    health-related behaviors
    such as diet, exercise, sleep
    cycles, and avoidance of
    substance abuse.

—. _____
    _____

—. _____
    _____

—. _____
    _____

DIAGNOSTIC SUGGESTIONS

Axis I:	307.89	Pain Disorder Associated with Both Psychological Factors and (Axis III Disorder)
	307.80	Pain Disorder Associated with Psychological Factors
	316	Psychological Factors Affecting (Axis III Disorder)
	300.81	Somatization Disorder
	304.80	Polysubstance Dependence
	_____	_____
	_____	_____

CIGARETTE SMOKING

BEHAVIORAL DEFINITIONS

1. Regular cigarette smoking that contributes to health problems.
2. Continued use of cigarettes despite experiencing persistent or recurring physical problems that are caused or exacerbated by smoking.
3. Use of tobacco in larger amounts and for longer periods than intended.
4. Increased tolerance for nicotine, manifested by either the absence of nausea or dizziness despite using substantial amounts or by the need for an increased amount to achieve the desired effect.
5. Experiencing physical withdrawal symptoms (e.g., restlessness, decreased heart rate, increased appetite, insomnia, anxiety, or irritability) within 24 hours of ceasing cigarette use.
6. Smoking upon waking or immediately upon leaving a smoking-restricted situation to avoid or relieve withdrawal symptoms.
7. Inability to quit smoking or decrease use of cigarettes, despite a verbalized desire to do so and/or previous unsuccessful attempts to quit.
8. Decreasing or suspending participation in important social, occupational, or recreational activities because they occur in smoking-restricted areas.
9. Lab work (i.e., blood, saliva, or urine sample test) that indicates high levels of nicotine or of its metabolite, cotinine.

__. _____
_____

__. _____
_____

__. _____
_____

LONG-TERM GOALS

1. Acquire the necessary skills to establish and maintain abstinence from smoking cigarettes.
2. Enhance confidence in ability to quit smoking, while increasing awareness of both the benefits of quitting and the health risks associated with continued smoking.
3. Develop coping strategies to deal with nicotine cravings and smoking cues in order to continue abstinence from smoking cigarettes.

—. _____

_____

—. _____

_____

—. _____

_____

SHORT-TERM OBJECTIVES

1. Describe history and current pattern of cigarette smoking. (1)

2. Cooperate with a physical exam to assess medical consequences of cigarette smoking. (2, 3)

3. Cooperate with adjunctive pharmacological treatment (e.g., nicotine replacement therapy or buproprion). (2, 3, 4)

4. Identify the negative ways that smoking has impacted life socially, emotionally, and physically. (5, 6, 7, 8)

5. Identify the potential benefits of quitting smoking. (6, 8, 9)

THERAPEUTIC INTERVENTIONS

1. Gather a history of patient's cigarette smoking as well as current use pattern.

2. Refer patient to physician for physical exam and for consideration of adjunctive pharmacological treatment.

3. Educate patient about nicotine-replacement therapy, including use of over-the-counter medications such as nicotine patch or nicotine gum.

4. Monitor patient's use of medications, including patient compliance and medication effectiveness. Confer with physician regarding prescription medications.

6. Verbalize an awareness of factors that have interfered with quitting smoking in the past. (10, 11)

7. Verbalize fears about degree of confidence in quitting smoking. (11, 12)

8. Verbalize how smoking behavior is at odds with broad, positive goals for life. (13)

9. Accurately self-monitor cigarette use by keeping a written record of each cigarette smoked and associated situational factors, thoughts, and feelings. (14)

10. Identify external cues for smoking (e.g., particular settings, activities, or interpersonal contexts associated with smoking behavior). (14, 15, 16)

11. Identify internal cues associated with smoking, including mood states, self-statements, and visual images. (14, 15, 17)

12. Practice at improving social interaction skills and report instances of less anxiety associated with the experience. (18, 19, 20)

13. Implement relaxation techniques to cope with anxiety that may trigger smoking. (21)

14. Identify negative, distorted self-talk that mediates anxiety, lack of confidence, or low self-esteem that can in turn trigger smoking. (22)

5. Educate patient about the health risks of smoking, including negative effects on the cardiovascular and respiratory systems.

6. Educate patient about the benefits of quitting smoking in terms of improved health and increased physical fitness.

7. Assist patient in identifying the negative impact smoking has had on life socially, emotionally, and physically.

8. Assign patient to read a self-help book or pamphlet on smoking cessation (e.g., American Cancer Society or American Lung Association pamphlet).

9. Assign patient to make a reasons-for-quitting list and to process it with therapist.

10. Assign patient to make a list of rationalizations previously used to maintain smoking habit.

11. Explore effective and ineffective strategies used by patient in previous efforts to quit smoking.

12. Explore patient's beliefs and fears about quitting smoking.

13. Explore patient's life goals and enhance awareness of the discrepancy between smoking behavior and broader life goals (e.g., maintaining good health, being physically fit).

15. Use positive self-talk to calm self and build confidence. (7, 17, 23)

16. List alternative behavioral activities to be used when the urge to smoke is strong. (24)

17. Calmly tell self that urge to smoke will pass. (17, 21, 25)

18. Implement stimulus-control techniques to control smoking behavior. (26, 27)

19. Identify rewards that would be effective in reinforcing abstinence. (28, 29)

20. Identify and utilize sources of positive social support in facilitating and maintaining abstinence from cigarette use. (30, 31)

21. Identify potential relapse triggers and verbalize a plan for dealing with them. (16, 17, 27, 32)

22. Verbalize a view of relapse as being a mistake that is a temporary setback versus a total failure. (33)

23. Verbalize a commitment to quit smoking on a specific date. (6, 9, 13, 34)

24. Agree to regular follow-up sessions to review progress and to discuss any further relapse prevention that may be necessary. (35)

14. Assign patient to maintain a diary of the number of cigarettes smoked per day and situational factors associated with smoking, including time of day, setting, activity, interpersonal context, thoughts, and emotions.

15. Process patient's diary information to identify smoking cues.

16. Assist patient in identifying people and situations that encourage or trigger smoking and discuss ways to cope with or avoid these situations.

17. Explore internal cues that trigger smoking (e.g., cognitions, negative emotions such as worry or anger, and self-statements) and assist patient in developing and implementing antismoking and pro-nonsmoking self-statements to use in response to these cues.

18. Use role playing, modeling, and behavioral rehearsal to teach patient social skills.

19. Refer patient to a social skills training group.

20. Train patient in assertiveness or refer to an assertiveness training class.

21. Teach patient relaxation techniques (e.g., progressive muscle relaxation, diaphragmatic breathing, or imagery) for coping with tension and anxiety that

__. _____
    _____

__. _____
    _____

__. _____
    _____

may trigger an urge to smoke.

22. Assist patient in identifying and modifying negative, distorted cognitions in response to stressors that contribute to negative effect.

23. Teach patient more realistic, positive self-talk and reinforce implementation of this self-enhancing skill.

24. Assign patient to generate a list of alternative activities and behaviors (e.g., chewing gum, exercising, talking to someone about urge, practicing deep breathing and relaxation) to utilize in response to the urge to smoke.

25. Teach patient use of coping phrases (e.g., "The urge will pass") in response to urges to smoke.

26. Teach patient stimulus-control techniques such as confining smoking only to particular places and/or times, and dissociating cigarette use from usual environmental cues for smoking.

27. Assist patient in constructing a hierarchy of settings and situations that trigger smoking. Assign patient to progressively eliminate smoking in each of these settings, starting with the easiest situation and gradually incorporating more difficult situations.

28. Assist patient in listing rewards that would reinforce abstinence.

29. Assist patient in setting up a self-reward system for reductions in cigarette use and for maintenance of abstinence.

30. Explore sources of social support available to patient in maintaining abstinence and discuss ways to develop and maintain a positive support system.

31. Encourage patient to involve and utilize significant other, friends, or family members as sources of support, encouragement, and positive reinforcement in effort to quit smoking.

32. Discuss potential relapse triggers and strategies for patient to effectively cope with them.

33. Educate patient on how to cope with lapses by cognitively reframing them as mistakes that can be used to prompt restorative coping strategies, rather than viewing a lapse as a failure that inevitably leads to a return to smoking habitually.

34. Assist patient in setting goals for the cessation of smoking, including identification of a target date for quitting.

35. Monitor patient's progress in cessation of smoking and modify supportive tech-

niques as necessary, reinforcing all successful efforts.

__. _____
  _____

__. _____
  _____

__. _____
  _____

DIAGNOSTIC SUGGESTIONS

Axis I: 305.10   Nicotine Dependence
       292.0   Nicotine Withdrawal
       292.9   Nicotine-Related Disorder NOS
       316   Maladaptive Health Behaviors Affecting (Axis
              III Disorder)

       _____   _____

       _____   _____

CYSTIC FIBROSIS (CF)

BEHAVIORAL DEFINITIONS

1. Abnormal mucous secretions that contribute to obstruction of the airways and chronic lung infections, ultimately causing loss of pulmonary function.
2. Respiratory symptoms, including coughing attacks and breathing difficulties.
3. Incomplete digestion and absorption of protein and fat.
4. Obstruction of pancreatic ducts, leading to abnormal electrolyte levels.
5. Delayed sexual development.
6. Sexual reproduction deficit (male sterility/female infertility).
7. Depression, helplessness, or hopelessness associated with chronic, terminal medical condition.
8. Feelings of anxiety associated with occurrence or anticipation of breathing difficulties.
9. Worry about respiratory symptoms that interferes with daily activities.
10. Emotional distress and coping difficulties associated with disease-related stressors (e.g., functional impairment, interpersonal concerns, time-consuming treatment regimen).
11. Poorly controlled disease-related pain that interferes with daily activities and restricts quality of life.
12. Noncompliance with medical treatment regimen.

__. _____
   _____
__. _____
   _____
__. _____
   _____

LONG-TERM GOALS

1. Increase knowledge about CF and medical treatment options.
2. Enhance sense of self-efficacy in managing CF.
3. Reduce fear, anxiety, and worry associated with medical condition.
4. Decrease feelings of depression and hopelessness.
5. Develop adaptive coping strategies for managing stressors and losses associated with chronic medical condition.
6. Reduce disruption in daily activities caused by respiratory symptoms.
7. Develop strategies to manage episodes of disease-related pain.
8. Achieve and maintain compliance with medical treatment regimen.

—. _____
   _____
   _____
—. _____
   _____
   _____
—. _____
   _____

SHORT-TERM OBJECTIVES

1. Provide history of medical condition and treatment regimen to the extent they are understood. (1, 4, 5, 10)

2. Verbalize increased knowledge about CF and treatment options. (2, 3, 18)

3. Comply with medical treatment regimen, reporting any problems or side effects to appropriate health care professionals. (4, 5, 6, 7)

4. Identify and utilize members of support system to help implement treatment regimen and disease-management behaviors. (8, 9, 10, 11)

THERAPEUTIC INTERVENTIONS

1. Explore patient's understanding of diagnosis, treatment options, and prognosis, while also assessing level of denial.

2. Assist patient and family members in obtaining information about CF from health care professionals, books and pamphlets, and reputable Internet sites.

3. Consult with patient's physician and other members of CF treatment team to enhance coordination of psychological and medical treatments.

5. Terminate "acting out" of anger or depression through noncompliance with treatment regimen. (12)

6. Implement dietary changes to maintain adequate level of nutrition. (13, 14)

7. Maintain regular pattern of exercise as medically recommended. (15)

8. Terminate the use of nicotine. (16)

9. Terminate the use or abuse of alcohol or illicit drugs. (17)

10. Attend a support group for individuals with CF. (18)

11. Implement strategies for improving communication with family members and addressing family stressors associated with demands of chronic illness. (12, 19)

12. Practice relaxation techniques daily to manage stress and anxiety and to create a more peaceful frame of mind. (20, 21, 22)

13. Develop and implement an action plan for coping with episodes of shortness of breath. (23, 24)

14. Implement coping strategies to reduce anxiety that interferes with ventilator weaning. (21, 23, 25)

15. Identify and verbally express feelings of anxiety and depression associated with medical condition. (23, 26)

4. Review patient's medical treatment regimen, including use of enzyme replacement therapy, oral antibiotics, aerosols and bronchodilators, other medications, and chest physiotherapy.

5. Assess patient's ability to understand medical instructions and care for self appropriately, identifying any developmental, emotional, or cognitive factors that may interfere.

6. Monitor and reinforce patient's compliance with medical treatment regimen, using behavioral contracting and goal setting to enhance compliance as needed.

7. Encourage patient to take active role in managing medical condition, as appropriate for developmental level (e.g., seeking information about CF, reporting disease-related symptoms and concerns, participating actively in treatment regimen).

8. Explore patient's support system, determining who is available to assist with critical disease-management behaviors and who is knowledgeable about what to do in a medical emergency.

9. Meet with family members to educate them regarding

16. Report to physicians or therapists any physical pain that causes concern or disrupts daily functioning. (27)

17. Implement coping strategies to manage pain episodes. (28)

18. Report to therapist any observed changes in memory, concentration, or thinking. (29)

19. Verbally express concerns and emotions associated with developmental, interpersonal, and transitional challenges and stressors associated with CF. (30, 31, 32)

20. Verbalize increased knowledge of safe birth-control methods and of the potential medical risks of pregnancy and childbirth. (33)

21. Identify life priorities and aspirations and implement a specific plan for achieving these goals. (34)

22. Verbalize a plan for managing future deterioration in physical health and use of life-support strategies. (35, 36)

23. Verbalize emotions associated with having a terminal medical condition and thoughts about approaching death. (26, 37, 38)

24. Identify ongoing stressors and implement changes in life situation to reduce stress. (39, 40)

their need to support patient's compliance with disease-management behaviors.

10. Review patient's and family members' level of confidence and knowledge in utilizing chest physiotherapy and postural drainage to clear mucous secretions.

11. Take necessary action to protect child with CF if family is unable or unwilling to provide adequate care and supervision in managing medical condition.

12. Actively intervene with individual and/or family therapy if adolescent with CF uses noncompliance with medical treatment as a form of "acting out."

13. Refer for consultation with nutritionist or dietician to address nutritional deficiencies resulting from patient's digestive abnormalities.

14. Intervene with behavioral strategies and/or refer for nutritional counseling to address patient's food avoidance secondary to nausea, indigestion, or cramping.

15. Monitor and reinforce patient's compliance with medically recommended exercise regimen.

16. Implement smoking cessation strategies with patient and family members, or

25. Verbalize increased acceptance of disease, while decreasing level of verbal denial. (1, 41)

26. Identify negatively biased, self-defeating cognitions. (41, 42, 43)

27. Replace irrational beliefs and distorted, negative cognitions with more realistic messages that reduce negative affect and promote a positive outlook. (44)

28. Identify enjoyable activities and incorporate them into daily life. (45, 46)

—. _____
    _____

—. _____
    _____

—. _____
    _____

refer for treatment of nicotine addiction.

17. Assess patient for substance abuse and refer for treatment of chemical dependency if indicated.

18. Refer patient and family members to a CF support group.

19. Provide family therapy to address stressors and adjustment issues associated with CF patient's medical condition.

20. Educate patient about the effects of anxiety and stress on respiratory symptoms.

21. Teach patient relaxation strategies such as imagery and deep-muscle relaxation to reduce stress and manage anxiety symptoms.

22. Utilize biofeedback training to enhance patient's development of relaxation techniques.

23. Explore patient's fears associated with breathing difficulties, ventilator weaning, or possible ventilator malfunction.

24. Help patient devise a plan for coping with episodes of shortness of breath (e.g., use of medication, oxygen, relaxation strategies).

25. Teach patient coping strategies (e.g., relaxation techniques, distraction) to reduce anxiety associated with weaning from ventilator during inpatient admission.

26. Assess and treat concomitant anxiety or depression. (See Anxiety and Depression chapters in this *Planner*.)

27. Assess patient for presence of pain associated with CF, including intensity, frequency, location, and quality of pain, as well as aggravating and relieving factors.

28. Help patient develop cognitive and behavioral coping strategies (e.g., positive imagery, positive self-talk, relaxation) for managing episodes of pain. (See Acute Pain and Chronic Pain chapters in this *Planner*.)

29. Monitor cognitive deficits secondary to insufficient oxygen and refer patient for neurological and/or neuropsychological assessment if indicated.

30. Explore patient's sexual development history and process emotions and concerns associated with delayed sexual development.

31. Assist adolescent or young adult with CF in addressing developmental challenges such as individuation from family, increasing level of independence, and academic/vocational transitions.

32. Explore patient's fears and concerns about marriage, ability to have children, and risks associated with having children.

33. Encourage sexually active patient to obtain medical advice regarding risks of pregnancy (i.e., with respect to patient's medical condition and the probability of genetic transmission of CF) and appropriate birth-control methods.

34. Explore patient's goals, hopes, and aspirations for the future (e.g., with respect to career, relationships, and/or personal growth) and assist in developing a plan for reaching these goals.

35. Encourage patient to clarify desires and preferences regarding end-of-life issues (e.g., decisions about withdrawal of life-sustaining treatment) with family members.

36. Assist patient and family members in anticipating and developing a plan for managing future decline in physical health.

37. Explore and process patient's fears about physical deterioration, death, and dying.

38. Normalize patient's feelings of grief, sadness, or anxiety associated with medical condition and encourage verbal expression of these emotions.

39. Assign patient to identify internal and external sources of daily stress.

40. Assist patient in developing coping strategies to address stressors (e.g., problem solving, communication skills, assertiveness training, anger management).

41. Encourage patient to develop a realistic outlook regarding symptoms and prognosis, while gently confronting the extremes of denial or an excessive focus on somatic symptoms.

42. Train patient to identify negative, self-defeating cognitions in response to stressful situations and disease-related concerns.

43. Assign patient to keep self-monitoring records of stressful events and accompanying cognitions and emotional reactions.

44. Teach patient to challenge and restructure dysfunctional, distorted thoughts by examining evidence for and against these cognitions and identifying alternative realistic interpretations.

45. Assist patient in developing rewarding and enjoyable activities to enhance life satisfaction.

46. Reinforce patient's involvement in social and recreational activities.

—. _____
    _____
—. _____
    _____
—. _____
    _____

DIAGNOSTIC SUGGESTIONS

Axis I: 316   Psychological Factors Affecting Cystic Fibrosis
              309.0   Adjustment Disorder with Depressed Mood
              309.24   Adjustment Disorder with Anxiety
              309.28   Adjustment Disorder with Mixed Anxiety and
                         Depressed Mood
              307.89   Pain Disorder Associated with Both
                         Psychological Factors and Cystic Fibrosis
              V15.81   Noncompliance with Treatment

              _____   _____
              _____   _____

DENTAL-RELATED PROBLEMS

BEHAVIORAL DEFINITIONS

1. Avoiding going to a dentist because of fear.
2. Neglecting going to a dentist because of indifference to long-term dental disease consequences.
3. Excessively elevated fear in anticipation of and during dental procedures.
4. A level of fear and agitation that complicates dentist's treatment efforts, usually increasing length of sessions.
5. Absence of behaviors (i.e., balanced nutrition, brushing, flossing, dental checkups) to prevent dental disease.
6. Clenching and grinding of teeth (bruxism), resulting in excessive tooth wear, pain, and possible temporomandibular disorders (TMD).
7. Chronic tensing of jaw musculature, resulting in pain and TMD.

—. _____
_____
_____

—. _____
_____
_____

—. _____
_____

LONG-TERM GOALS

1. Establish pattern of regular dental checkups and care.
2. Make decisions regarding dental care unimpeded by phobic anxiety.
3. Take increased responsibility for proper care of teeth and gums.
4. Tolerate dental examination or treatment without disruptive anxiety.

5. Eliminate (or at least reduce) bruxism and muscle clenching of jaw.

—. _____

_____

—. _____

_____

—. _____

_____

SHORT-TERM OBJECTIVES

1. Describe history of dental problems and dental treatment. (1, 2)

2. Acknowledge the actual or potential negative consequences of neglecting dental care. (3, 4)

3. Increase knowledge of dental disease and how to prevent dental problems. (4, 5, 6)

4. Demonstrate increased responsibility by consistently cleaning teeth and gums, with daily brushing and regular flossing. (4, 7, 10)

5. Demonstrate responsibility by self-examining gums, maintaining healthy diet, avoiding foods particularly hazardous to teeth (e.g., chewing tobacco or hard candy), and keeping dental appointments. (5, 6, 7, 10)

6. Stop verbalizing excuses for not going to the dentist and agree to schedule regular dental care. (8, 9, 10)

THERAPEUTIC INTERVENTIONS

1. Gather history of patient's dental problems, dental care, and attitudes toward care of teeth and gums.

2. Explore and encourage talk about patient's traumatic dental experiences, especially during childhood.

3. Discuss links between healthy teeth and gums, facial appearance, and positive self-concept.

4. Help patient become sensitive to long-term negative consequences of neglecting dental hygiene (e.g., tooth pain, impaired chewing of food, negative impact on appearance, increased costs of treating serious dental and gum problems).

5. Teach patient that more tooth loss is due to periodontal (gum) disease than to decay.

6. Provide patient with pamphlets, videotapes, or reliable Internet sites that give

7. Sign a release of information document to allow therapist to coordinate care with dentist and/or dental hygienist. (11)

8. Identify distorted, negative automatic thoughts that generate fear and avoidance of dental treatment. (12)

9. Implement the use of positive self-talk to reduce anxiety related to dental treatment. (13, 15)

10. Use relaxation techniques to control pain and reduce emotional reactivity during dental treatment. (14, 15)

11. Cooperate with systematic desensitization of anxiety-related stimuli. (16, 17, 18)

12. Implement relaxation strategies for TMD. (14, 19)

13. Take psychotropic medication as prescribed. (20, 21)

14. Model appropriate attitudes and behaviors toward dental care to prevent own child from developing dental phobia and to help the child develop positive attitudes toward dentistry. (22)

—. _____
   _____

—. _____
   _____

—. _____
   _____

information about tooth and gum care and disease consequences related to lack of dental hygiene and/or poor nutritional habits.

7. Develop behavioral self-monitoring plan for patient's daily tooth and gum care and reinforce adherence.

8. Assist patient with following the necessary steps for proper dental care.

9. Refer patient to a dentist who is skilled in working with anxious patients and who is concerned with pain management.

10. Reinforce emotional stability, behavioral responsibility, and positive self-talk by patient regarding dental care.

11. Consult with patient's dentist and dental hygienist to develop an individual behavioral plan for helping to overcome fear through behavioral/cognitive coping strategies and possible use of psychotropic medications.

12. Assist patient in identifying those negative cognitions that feed fear and avoidance of dental treatment.

13. Help patient develop healthy, realistic self-talk to replace negative automatic thoughts as a means of reducing anxiety related to dental treatment.

14. Instruct patient in the use of psychophysiologic self-relaxation skills (i.e., focused attention, deep/slow breathing, deep-muscle relaxation, hand warming) to control pain and reduce emotional reaction during dental treatment.

15. Instruct patient in covert cognitive rehearsal (i.e., imagine viewing oneself successfully using self-relaxation, positive self-talk, and other coping skills during uncomfortable dental procedure).

16. Assist patient in creating a hierarchy of anxiety-producing situations related to dental office visits and treatment procedures.

17. Use systematic desensitization procedure with imagery presentation of hierarchy items while patient is deeply relaxed.

18. Accompany patient to dental office for practicing *in vivo* desensitization and coping skills.

19. Conduct or refer for EMG biofeedback to assist patient in learning muscle relaxation to control clenching and bruxing.

20. Refer patient for evaluation for prescription for psychotropic medication to treat phobic anxiety or if bruxing is severe.

21. Monitor patient for medication compliance, effectiveness, and possible side effects.

22. Discuss importance of modeling and encouragement in helping children develop positive attitudes and behaviors regarding care of teeth and gums.

—. _____

_____

—. _____

_____

—. _____

_____

DIAGNOSTIC SUGGESTIONS

Axis I: 300.29   Specific Phobia
308.3   Acute Stress Disorder
309.81   Posttraumatic Stress Disorder
300.02   Generalized Anxiety Disorder
316   Psychological Factors Affecting (Axis III Disorder)

_____   _____

_____   _____

DEPRESSION RELATED TO MEDICAL PROBLEMS

BEHAVIORAL DEFINITIONS

1. Unresolved feelings of grief, worthlessness, or sadness associated with medical condition and decline in daily functioning.
2. Feelings of hopelessness or helplessness associated with medical condition.
3. Depressed affect.
4. Diminished interest in or enjoyment of activities.
5. Psychomotor agitation or retardation.
6. Sleeplessness or hypersomnia.
7. Lack of energy.
8. Loss of appetite.
9. Poor concentration or indecisiveness.
10. Social withdrawal.
11. Suicidal thoughts and/or gestures.
12. Low self-esteem.
13. History of chronic or recurrent depression for which patient has taken antidepressant medication, been hospitalized, had outpatient treatment, or had a course of electroconvulsive therapy.

__. _____

_____

__. _____

_____

__. _____

_____

LONG-TERM GOALS

1. Appropriately grieve changes in health status and achieve an adaptive level of functioning.
2. Cope effectively with medical condition and associated life changes.
3. Recognize, accept, and cope with feelings of depression.
4. Alleviate depressed mood and return to previous level of effective functioning.
5. Develop healthy cognitive patterns and beliefs about self and the world that lead to alleviation of depressive symptoms.
6. Improve ability to identify and express emotions associated with medical condition.

—. _____
   _____
   _____
—. _____
   _____
   _____
—. _____
   _____

SHORT-TERM OBJECTIVES

1. Describe the signs and symptoms of depression that are experienced. (1, 2)

2. Verbally identify, if possible, the source(s) of depressed mood. (2, 3, 4)

3. Identify emotional effects of medical condition. (3, 4, 5, 27)

4. Begin to experience sadness in session while discussing disappointment or grief associated with changes in health and daily functioning. (4, 5, 6)

THERAPEUTIC INTERVENTIONS

1. Explore symptoms of depression and how they are experienced in patient's day-to-day living.

2. Encourage patient to share feelings of depression in order to clarify them and gain insight as to causes.

3. Explore the emotional impact of life changes associated with patient's medical condition.

4. Process patient's feelings of grief and loss associated with changes in health and lifestyle.

5. Verbalize fears about deterioration in health that could lead to significantly reduced functioning or even death. (6)

6. Verbalize an understanding of the relationship between depressed mood and repression of feelings (e.g., anger, hurt, fear, grief). (7)

7. Complete psychological testing to assess severity of depression and possible need for antidepressant medication or suicide-prevention measures. (8)

8. Take medication as prescribed by physician and report any side effects to physician or therapist. (9, 10)

9. Express feelings of hurt, disappointment, shame, and anger associated with early life experiences. (11)

10. Show evidence of daily personal grooming and hygiene, with minimal reminders from others. (12)

11. Engage in physical and recreational activities that reflect increased energy and interest. (13, 22, 30, 31)

12. Identify cognitive self-talk that contributes to and maintains depression. (14, 15)

13. Become more aware of negative self-talk by keeping self-monitoring records of automatic negative

5. Normalize patient's feelings of grief, sadness, or fear associated with medical condition and encourage verbal expression of these emotions.

6. Explore and process patient's fears about deterioration of physical health, dying, and death.

7. Explain a connection between repressed emotions and patient's current depressive symptomatology.

8. Arrange for administration of Minnesota Multiphasic Inventory-2, Beck Depression Inventory, Modified Scale for Suicidal Ideation, or other assessment instruments. Evaluate results and give feedback to patient.

9. Refer patient to a physician for physical examination to rule out organic causes of depression and to assess need for antidepressant medication.

10. Monitor patient's medication compliance and the effectiveness of medications on level of functioning.

11. Explore childhood experiences that contribute to patient's current depressed state.

12. Monitor and redirect patient in maintaining daily grooming and hygiene.

13. Assist patient in developing a plan for increasing partic-

thoughts in response to stressors. (15)

14. Replace negative and self-defeating self-talk with realistic and positive cognitive messages. (15, 16, 18, 19)

15. Verbalize hopeful and positive statements regarding the future. (17, 18, 19)

16. Make positive statements about self and ability to cope with medical condition. (16, 18, 19, 24)

17. Share with therapist any history of suicide attempts and current suicidal urges. (20, 21)

18. Report no longer having thoughts of harming self. (16, 19, 22)

19. Participate in social contacts and initiate communication of needs and desires. (22, 26, 29)

20. Identify and implement strategies to enhance sense of control in dealing with medical condition. (23, 24, 25)

21. Attend a support group related to medical condition and discuss emotional impact of attending with therapist. (26)

22. Keep a journal of feelings about medical condition and associated life changes. (27)

23. Read books on overcoming depression, and discuss insights and reactions with therapist. (28)

ipation in recreational activities.

14. Assist patient in developing awareness of cognitive messages that reinforce helplessness and hopelessness.

15. Assign patient to keep a record of daily events and associated dysfunctional cognitions and emotions. Challenge dysfunctional thoughts for accuracy, and identify alternative cognitive interpretations that are more positive and realistic.

16. Reinforce positive, reality-based cognitive messages that enhance patient's self-confidence and increase adaptive action.

17. Educate patient about depression and accepting some sadness as a normal variation in feeling.

18. Assign patient to write at least one positive affirmation statement daily regarding self and the future.

19. Verbally reinforce patient's positive self-statements.

20. Explore patient's history of suicidal ideation and behavior and assess current suicide potential.

21. Arrange for hospitalization, as necessary, when patient is judged to be a threat to self.

22. Reinforce patient's participation in social activities and verbalization of feelings, needs, and desires.

24. Increase frequency of assertive behaviors to express needs, desires, and expectations. (22, 29)

25. Participate in exercise as recommended by physician. (30)

—. _____
_____

—. _____
_____

—. _____
_____

23. Help patient implement strategies that enhance sense of control in managing medical condition (e.g., taking an active role in treatment plan, seeking information to increase knowledge about medical condition).

24. Challenge patient to focus on capabilities rather than disabilities.

25. Assist patient in developing skills (e.g., relaxation techniques, communication skills, decreased internal focus, problem solving) to enhance coping with medical condition.

26. Refer patient to a support group related to medical condition.

27. Assign patient to keep a journal of emotions about losses and life changes due to medical condition. Process during treatment sessions.

28. Recommend self-help books on coping with depression (e.g., *The Feeling Good Handbook* by Burns, *What to Say When You Talk to Yourself* by Helmstetter, or *Talking to Yourself* by Butler).

29. Teach patient assertiveness skills, using modeling, behavioral rehearsal, and role playing.

30. Encourage and reinforce patient's participation in medically appropriate exercise.

31. Recommend that patient read *Exercising Your Way to Better Mental Health* (Leith).

___. _____

_____

___. _____

_____

___. _____

_____

DIAGNOSTIC SUGGESTIONS

Axis I:

309.0	Adjustment Disorder with Depressed Mood
296.2x	Major Depressive Disorder, Single Episode
296.3x	Major Depressive Disorder, Recurrent
296.xx	Bipolar I Disorder
296.89	Bipolar II Disorder
300.4	Dysthymic Disorder
301.13	Cyclothymic Disorder
295.70	Schizoaffective Disorder
293.83	Mood Disorder Due to (Axis III Disorder)
316	Psychological Factors Affecting (Axis III Disorder)
_____	_____
_____	_____

DIABETES

BEHAVIORAL DEFINITIONS

1. Unable to properly use and store glucose (or "sugar") due to inadequate insulin production by the pancreas.
2. Failure to control the disease because of insufficient effort or skill at self-monitoring and controlling of blood glucose.
3. Failure of parents or guardians to properly and consistently help their child or adolescent with juvenile-onset diabetes to learn how to control level of blood glucose through appropriate diet, exercise, and use of medication.
4. Continued harmful behaviors (e.g., faulty diet, lack of exercise, smoking, excessive alcohol consumption, poor weight control) despite knowledge of risks for a diabetic person.
5. Inattention to the acute warning signs (e.g., frequent thirst and urination, blurred vision, poor wound healing) that blood glucose levels are too high (hyperglycemia) or too low (hypoglycemia).
6. Lack of proper understanding and/or concern about long-term risk factors (e.g., blindness, kidney failure, impaired circulation) associated with poor glucose control.
7. Mood state instability associated with widely fluctuating glucose levels.
8. Depression and anxiety secondary to lack of acceptance of the disease and/or complications brought on by the disease.

—. _____
_____

—. _____
_____

—. _____
_____

LONG-TERM GOALS

1. Become as knowledgeable as possible about all aspects of living with diabetes.
2. Develop confidence in ability to use knowledge about diabetes to maintain blood glucose levels in desired range and thus minimize short- and long-term complications.
3. Learn how to accurately use monitors for self-measurement of blood glucose (SMBG) and to recognize subjective symptoms of glucose fluctuations.
4. Be aware that diabetes is potentially a serious life-threatening disorder, but minimize fearfulness by careful attention to proper management.
5. Engage in long-term health maintenance behaviors known to reduce risks associated with diabetes.
6. Live as normal and full life as possible through proper management rather than trying to ignore or forget about the condition.
7. Family members and close friends gain information on how to provide assistance in case of hypoglycemic emergency.

—. _____

_____

—. _____

_____

—. _____

_____

SHORT-TERM OBJECTIVES

1. Study information about diabetes and verbalize increased knowledge about living with this disease. (1, 2, 3)

2. Establish a target glucose level that will trigger self-administration of insulin. (1, 2, 3)

3. Demonstrate reliable self-measurement of blood glucose (SMBG). (3)

THERAPEUTIC INTERVENTIONS

1. Assist patient in obtaining verbal and written information from sources such as physicians, diabetes nurse educator, dietician, or The American Diabetes Association (www.diabetes.org/default.htm).

2. Recommend educational resources that communicate at patient's level of understanding—especially if pa-

4. Verbalize when to implement SMBG, following the guidelines established with medical treatment team. (3, 4)

5. Demonstrate the ability for self-administration of insulin injections. (2, 3, 4)

6. Keep insulin easily available at all times. (1, 4)

7. Keep food or drink source containing glucose easily available in case of becoming hypoglycemic. (1, 5)

8. Verbalize an understanding of critical behaviors that must be regularly implemented to manage diabetes and its complications. (6)

9. Identify disease-management behaviors that are most resistant to implementation. (7)

10. Set goals and agree to a contract that will increase compliance with resistant critical disease-management behaviors. (7, 8)

11. Monitor diet and plan meals that will facilitate weight control and maintain proper blood glucose levels. (8, 9)

12. Follow an exercise program that will promote glucose management via weight control and general fitness. (6, 8, 9)

13. Identify the body's unique glucose patterns and determine what causes blood glucose changes. (1, 2, 3, 6, 10)

tient has reading, comprehension, or other cognitive or emotional deficits that might impair learning self-care skills.

3. Refer to a diabetes educator who can train and check patient's accuracy in SMBG as well as teach patient how to set a target glucose level and how to take corrective action for controlling glucose.

4. Review patient's degree of confidence and knowledge regarding self-administration of insulin.

5. Encourage and reward responsible self-management of blood glucose.

6. Review with patient a diabetic behavioral checklist that includes critical behaviors that must be implemented regularly (e.g., SMBG, use of insulin or diabetes medication, meal planning, exercise, foot care, sickday management, and periodic testing of eyes, kidneys, and blood pressure).

7. Encourage patient to identify from checklist of critical disease-management behaviors areas where compliance may be difficult.

8. Develop behavioral plan (e.g., goal setting and behavioral contracting) for improving compliance with critical disease-management behaviors.

14. Terminate the use or abuse of alcohol or nicotine so as to better manage blood glucose levels. (1, 11, 12, 13)

15. Verbalize cognitive, mood, and sensory changes that may reflect fluctuating blood glucose. (14, 15)

16. Verbalize feelings of depression or anxiety that accompany adaptation to diabetes. (16)

17. Ensure that significant others in the patient's household demonstrate knowledge regarding disease management and how to respond in case of a blood glucose emergency. (17, 18, 19)

18. Terminate "acting out" of anger or depression through noncompliance with critical disease-management behaviors. (18, 19, 20)

19. Wear bracelet identifying diabetic condition. (21)

20. Verbalize an understanding of the special care required in managing sickness or accidents (e.g., watch for drug interactions). (1, 6, 22)

21. Verbalize an understanding of the need for special prenatal care if a pregnancy occurs. (23)

22. Verbalize an understanding of the effect of mood state and stress on blood glucose levels. (16, 24)

9. Provide patient with diet, exercise, and weight control advice or refer for diet consultation with physician and/or nutritionist. Develop behavior modification program with patient to address diet and weight control compliance.

10. Assist patient in identifying his/her unique glucose patterns and those factors (e.g., diet, exercise, stress, alcohol, or nicotine use) that lead to blood glucose changes.

11. Review the special physiological dangers of substance abuse (including tobacco and alcohol) in patient who is diabetic, encouraging abstinence.

12. Refer patient for substance abuse treatment to facilitate abstinence and greater blood glucose control.

13. Develop a stop-smoking program (see Smoking chapter of this *Planner*) or refer patient for treatment of nicotine addiction.

14. Review and assist patient in identifying those physical, cognitive, and emotional changes that may be reflective of poorly controlled blood glucose.

15. Recognize and intervene where acute or chronic neuropsychological cognitive impairments (whether or not a direct result of diabetic condition) may impair capacity for self-management.

23. Reduce those sources of stress that can reasonably be changed or avoided. (25)

24. Identify automatic thoughts that trigger debilitating emotional responses to stress. (26)

25. Increase use of positive self-talk in response to daily sources of stress. (27)

26. Use self-relaxation skills involving breath control, muscle relaxation, and mental imagery to manage stress. (28, 29, 30)

—. _____
   _____

—. _____
   _____

—. _____
   _____

16. Assess patient for depression and anxiety, and treat as necessary. (See Depression and Anxiety chapters in this *Planner*.)

17. Explore patient's support system, determining who is available to help with critical disease-management behavior compliance and who is knowledgeable about what to do in a glucose emergency.

18. Meet with and educate family members regarding their need to support compliance with disease-management behavior and to provide emergency aid if patient's blood glucose unmanageability results in a coma or other medical crisis.

19. Take necessary action to protect child with diabetes from ravages of poor glucose management if family is unable or unwilling to provide adequate care and supervision.

20. Actively intervene with individual and family therapy if adolescent with diabetes uses noncompliance glucose management as a form of "acting out."

21. Emphasize to patient the potential lifesaving value of always wearing a medical alert bracelet identifying the diabetic condition, and reinforce compliance.

22. Educate patient regarding the special steps that must be taken to manage diabetes during sickness and vomiting or in case of accidental injury.

23. Encourage seeking of immediate medical consultation if a diabetic patient (or a patient with a family history of diabetes) suspects that she is pregnant. (Blood glucose and urine ketones must be carefully monitored during pregnancy.)

24. Teach patient about possible effects of stress on glucose levels and insulin requirements.

25. Aid patient in recognizing sources of environmental stress and in reducing those that can be changed.

26. Encourage and assist patient in recognizing dysfunctional automatic thoughts and emotional response patterns that may contribute to high levels of stress.

27. Teach and reinforce positive realistic, cognitive self-talk as a means of coping with stress.

28. Teach patient how to use cognitive and somatic self-relaxation techniques such as breath control, muscle relaxation, and visual imagery.

29. Use biofeedback to train patient in deep-muscle relaxation.

30. Alert patient practicing relaxation skills to be sensitive to possible changes in
insulin requirements, since
studies have demonstrated
that relaxation training can
reduce insulin requirements
in individuals with dia-
betes.

__. _____
_____
__. _____
_____
__. _____
_____

DIAGNOSTIC SUGGESTIONS

Axis I:

316	Psychological Factors Affecting Diabetes
V71.09	No Diagnosis or Condition on Axis I
V15.81	Noncompliance with Treatment
294.1	Dementia Due to Diabetes
309.0	Adjustment Disorder with Depressed Mood
309.24	Adjustment Disorder with Anxiety
309.3	Adjustment Disorder with Disturbance of Conduct
_____	_____
_____	_____

EPILEPSY

BEHAVIORAL DEFINITIONS

1. Recurrent seizures that are characterized by unusual sensations or hallucinations.
2. Recurrent seizures that are characterized by episodes of cognitive confusion.
3. Recurrent seizures that are characterized by convulsions.
4. Seizures disturb ongoing cognitive and motor functioning to such a degree that there is a risk of injury to self or others (e.g., while driving).
5. Seizures are cause of fear of reoccurrence.
6. Depression, anxiety, obsessive-compulsive and phobic behavior linked to epilepsy.
7. Cognitive and behavioral signs of brain dysfunction.

—. _____
   _____
   _____
—. _____
   _____
—. _____
   _____

LONG-TERM GOALS

1. Reduce the frequency and severity of epileptic seizures as much as possible.
2. Ensure personal safety of self and others as much as possible.
3. Establish appropriate antiseizure medication routine with physician and be compliant with this routine.

4. Become as knowledgeable and self-reliant as possible in management of condition.
5. Minimize impact of symptoms on daily activities as much as possible.
6. Understand, avoid, and control exposure to known seizure triggers whenever possible.

__. _____
   _____
   _____
__. _____
   _____
   _____
__. _____
   _____

SHORT-TERM OBJECTIVES

1. Describe the nature and frequency of seizures. (1)
2. Verbalize an increased understanding about the medical condition of epilepsy. (2, 3)
3. Verbalize confidence in the treating physician. (4)
4. Maintain perfect compliance in taking prescribed antiepilepsy medication. Make changes in medication use only after full discussion with physician. (4, 5)
5. Verbalize a rational understanding of the importance of both short-term and long-term control of seizures. (4, 5, 6)
6. Wear a bracelet or other identification that identifies the condition. (7)

THERAPEUTIC INTERVENTIONS

1. Explore the type and frequency of the seizures that the patient experiences.
2. Explore patient's understanding and beliefs about epilepsy.
3. Assist patient in obtaining verbal and written information about epilepsy (e.g., Epilepsy Foundation of America at web site www.efa.org).
4. Discuss patient's relationship with doctors. Encourage development of trusting relationship with a neurologist.
5. Assist the patient in maintaining compliance with prescribed antiepilepsy medication. Set up medication self-monitoring program if necessary.

7. Participate in neuropsychological testing if recommended. (8)

8. Keep a log of seizure activity, including date, time, environmental circumstances, emotional status, and stress level prior to seizure onset. (9)

9. Verbalize an understanding of sensory and emotional situations that can lower seizure threshold. (10)

10. State steps that will be taken to avoid stimuli such as pulsating sounds and blinking lights that may be seizure triggers. (10, 11, 12)

11. Terminate the use of alcohol or illicit drugs that can reduce seizure threshold. (13, 14)

12. Verbalize a plan to minimize bodily status risk factors (e.g., dehydration, hyperventilation, or fatigue). (15)

13. Inform others of seizure condition to avoid endangering self or others. (16, 17, 18, 19)

14. Verbalize confidence with challenging the misinformation and prejudice that may be encountered in others in response to diagnosis of epilepsy. (18, 19)

15. Report any reduction in those anxieties and fears about epilepsy that may have led to overrestriction of daily life activities. (2, 3, 20)

6. Teach the patient the importance of and the means to short- and long-term control of seizures.

7. Encourage patient to always wear a bracelet or have some other identification that clearly identifies medical condition of epilepsy.

8. Refer patient for neuropsychological assessment if signs of neuropsychological dysfunction are present.

9. Encourage patient to maintain a seizure log. Review log with patient to spot trends in circumstances (e.g., date, time, environmental circumstances, emotional status, stress level) preceding onset of seizures.

10. Teach patient the concept of sensory stimuli that may trigger seizures as well as other circumstances that may lower seizure threshold.

11. Discuss behaviors required to reduce exposure to specific stimuli (e.g., blinking lights and pulsating music) that may trigger seizures.

12. Teach family and teachers that patient may behaviorally induce seizures by such actions as fluttering eyes or waving of hands in front of eyes.

13. Assess patient for alcohol and/or drug dependency

16. Verbalize acceptance of those restrictions that are necessary for safety (e.g., not driving unless seizures are effectively and consistently controlled). (7, 20, 21)

17. Verbalize an understanding of the relationship between stress reactivity and seizure occurrence. (22, 23)

18. Identify sources of external or environmental stress. (24)

19. Develop and implement a plan for reducing sources of external stress. (25, 26)

20. Verbalize feelings of depression, anxiety, and anger that may result from epilepsy or any other source. (22, 27)

21. Report more controlled emotional reactions to stressful situations. (22, 27, 28, 33, 34)

22. Identify automatic thoughts that can trigger negative emotional responses. (29, 30)

23. Increase the use of positive self-talk in response to stressful situations. (31)

24. Practice the cognitive skill of focusing attention on mental imagery to initiate self-regulation of mind and body. (32)

25. Practice relaxation skills. (33, 34, 35)

26. Implement self-regulation to achieve mental calmness. (36)

that can precipitate seizures.

14. Discuss with patient behaviors required to terminate exposure to alcohol and various drugs and drug mixtures that could reduce seizure threshold.

15. Teach patient the behaviors required to prevent specific physical risk factors (e.g., dehydration, hyperventilation, excessive fatigue) that could reduce seizure thresholds.

16. Explore with patient the pros and cons of revealing epilepsy status to specific people.

17. Encourage patient to provide family and selected members of social network with basic seizure first-aid information.

18. Employ rationale-emotive therapy and desensitization to help patient confront and overcome embarrassment over epilepsy.

19. Discuss with patient the range of behavioral and even legal strategies for dealing with prejudice and discrimination against persons with epilepsy.

20. Encourage the patient, while always maintaining a proper concern for safety, to not overrestrict activity out of fear of a possible seizure.

27. Report success in using self-regulation in coping with stressful situations in daily life. (36, 37)

28. Report on the social/behavioral consequences of seizure activity. (38, 39)

—. _____
   _____

—. _____
   _____

—. _____
   _____

21. Reinforce the adherence to driving restrictions until seizures are consistently eliminated for the medically stipulated time.

22. Promote patient's understanding of mind-body relationships via discussion of concepts of coping, stress-management, and possible relationship with seizure activity.

23. Promote patient's understanding of the concept of stress, making a distinction between external and internal sources of stress and between cognitive and physiological manifestations of stress.

24. Help the patient to recognize sources of environmental stress.

25. Assist the patient in developing a plan for changing or eliminating those sources of external stress that can be modified.

26. Provide or refer for specific types of problem-focused counseling (e.g., marital, vocational, financial) as needed.

27. Explore with patient strong emotional reactions to external stress that may lower seizure threshold.

28. Use role playing, modeling, and behavioral rehearsal to teach the patient controlled, calm, modulated reaction to stressful situations.

29. Teach the patient how negative cognitive distortions can lead to feelings of fear, anger, and depression.

30. Assist the patient in identifying distorted automatic thoughts that trigger negative emotions.

31. Teach and reinforce positive realistic self-talk as a means of coping with stress.

32. Assist the patient in developing the cognitive skills of focused attention and visualization as prerequisite tools for learning psychophysiological self-regulation. Help the patient identify and overcome blocks to using these skills.

33. Teach the patient how to use self-relaxation skills such as slow/deep breathing, deep-muscle relaxation, and hand/foot warming.

34. Use biofeedback as an aid in psychophysiological self-regulation training. (Caution: If EEG biofeedback is used, make sure therapist has the required specialized expertise to treat epilepsy.)

35. Provide patient with cassette tapes and written material for home practice of self-regulation skills.

36. Help patient in using visualization and physiological self-regulation to achieve internal state of mental calmness.

37. Assist patient in developing use of psychophysiological self-regulation as an adaptive coping skill in a wide variety of specific situations.

38. Especially with children and adolescents, do a behavioral analysis of seizure contingencies (i.e., positive and negative consequences of the seizures).

39. In hospital or other institutional setting for children and adolescents, develop a reward system contingent on time period without seizure.

__. _____
    _____

__. _____
    _____

__. _____
    _____

DIAGNOSTIC SUGGESTIONS:

Axis I:

	310.1	Personality Change Due to Epilepsy
	293.9	Mental Disorder NOS Due to Epilepsy
	294.0	Amnestic Disorder Due to Epilepsy
	293.89	Anxiety Disorder Due to Epilepsy
	311	Depressive Disorder NOS
	299.80	Pervasive Developmental Disorder NOS
	_____	_____
	_____	_____

FIBROMYALGIA

BEHAVIORAL DEFINITIONS

1. Chronic diffuse aching and stiffness of muscles and connective tissues, often throughout much of the body.
2. Weakness of muscles and/or areas of tenderness ("trigger points") that when touched can radiate pain to other points in the body.
3. Reports of a feeling of swelling, although described condition cannot be seen by others.
4. Poor-quality, nonrestorative sleep leading to feelings of extreme fatigue.
5. Reduction in normal activities but without complete loss of functional capacity.
6. Mild to severe depressed mood.
7. Poor communication and high frustration level with health professionals, who may not take diagnosis seriously.
8. Frequent changes in health care providers.
9. Overreliance on various medications (i.e., analgesics, anti-inflammatory, antibiotic), often with little benefit.
10. Irritability and disturbed interpersonal relationships with family, friends, and employers.

—. _____
_____

—. _____
_____

—. _____
_____

LONG-TERM GOALS

1. Reduce the chronic discomfort of aching muscles.
2. Become as knowledgeable and self-reliant as possible in management of the medical condition.
3. Demonstrate improved coping with pain as reflected in maintenance or restoration of functioning.
4. Become an active partner with treatment specialists, restricting "doctor-shopping," and accepting the limits of medical knowledge in the diagnosis and treatment of this condition.
5. Actively strive to live as normal a life as possible even if discomfort and fatigue are present.
6. Maintain rewarding relationships with others.
7. Use medications with caution, terminating the use of medicines and other treatments that seem to provide no improvement.
8. Recognize the importance of mind-body relationships (e.g., the links between pain, poor sleep, and depressed mood).
9. Practice positive thinking that avoids a preoccupation with symptoms.
10. Develop and implement behavioral and psychophysiologic self-regulation skills for pain, depression, and sleep management.

—. _____

_____

—. _____

_____

—. _____

_____

SHORT-TERM OBJECTIVES	THERAPEUTIC INTERVENTIONS
1. Acquire information and verbalize increased knowledge about the perplexing medical condition of fibromyalgia. (1)	1. Explore the patient's understanding of fibromyalgia and provide direction for obtaining verbal and written information about condition from sources such as health care professionals, books, pamphlets, articles, and reputable Internet sites.
2. Establish a trusting relationship with an understanding physician. (2)	

3. Avoid doctors and other therapists who "overtreat" or promise "too much." (3)

4. Verbalize acceptance of the fact that condition is poorly understood by medical science and thus difficult to diagnose and treat. (1, 3)

5. Strive daily to focus on what activities can be engaged in rather than on activities that cannot be done. (4, 5, 33)

6. Verbalize an understanding of the difference between benign symptoms and imaginary symptoms. (6)

7. Set specific health-improvement goals, rather than vague health-related goals. (7, 8)

8. Report improved sleep pattern after implementing behavioral sleep techniques. (9, 17)

9. Agree to pace self, and verbalize a plan on how to best manage activities. (5, 10, 33)

10. Develop enjoyable substitutes for activities that are no longer possible. (4, 5, 10, 11)

11. Increase amount of daily physical exercise as a means of building physical strength, reducing stress, and improving mood. (12, 13, 17)

12. Change to a diet that is balanced in the five major food groups and eat meals on a

2. Discuss with patient his/her relationship with doctors. If necessary, refer patient to a physician who takes a positive approach to management of fibromyalgia.

3. Consistently caution the patient to be realistic in expectations regarding the speed of recovery or completeness of treatment success.

4. Challenge patient's beliefs and misinformation that encourage passivity, bed rest, and/or long-term inactivity as helpful in relieving fibromyalgia.

5. Challenge patient for putting life on "hold" until finding a cure for symptoms. Encourage acceptance of management of symptoms.

6. Help the patient appreciate the difference between benign symptoms and "imaginary" symptoms.

7. Promote talk about specific feasible goals rather than vague wishes or desires such as wanting to "feel better" or wishing to have "more energy."

8. Acquaint patient with the concepts of health promotion, rather than just focusing on symptom relief.

9. Encourage the patient to use behavioral sleep techniques (e.g., retire at the same time each night, uti-

regular daily schedule.
(14, 15, 16, 17)

13. Verbalize an understanding of the link between emotional/attitudinal state and physical symptoms. (18, 19, 20)

14. Verbalize an understanding that inactivity, boredom, and/or lack of making a contribution to life can lead to depression. (11, 12, 13, 20, 21)

15. Verbalize feelings of depression and anxiety that may contribute to pain and fatigue. (20, 22)

16. Identify automatic thoughts that can trigger negative emotional responses. (23, 24)

17. Increase use of positive self-talk in response to pain and stress. (25)

18. Identify past or current experiences of physical, sexual, or emotional abuse. (22, 26)

19. Verbalize ways to reduce frustration and manage anger toward those who seem critical and unsupportive. (27)

20. Learn and use psychophysiologic self-relaxation skills (i.e., slow-deep breathing, muscle relaxation, hand warming) to aid in management of pain and stress. (28, 29, 30)

21. Practice self-induced analgesia. (31)

lize relaxation skills, warm bath before bed, avoid spices or caffeine in diet).

10. Encourage and reinforce the planning of activities to minimize overexertion and/or activity avoidance.

11. Assign the patient to list a substitute activity for every activity that he/she claims cannot be engaged in due to discomfort.

12. Assist the patient in developing a routine of daily physical exercise.

13. Recommend that the patient read and implement programs from *Exercising Your Way to Better Mental Health* by Leith.

14. Assist the patient in planning meals that are balanced to give adequate nutrition and improve health and energy.

15. Refer the patient to a dietician for meal planning and dietary education.

16. Urge the patient to eat meals on a regular schedule to promote routine in eating, sleeping, and activity.

17. Monitor patient's diet, times of eating, exercise, and sleep cycle, refocusing behavior as necessary.

18. Raise the patient's awareness of mind-body relationships.

19. Aid the patient in separating physical discomfort from emotional suffering.

22. Reduce the level of and re-activity to environmental stress. (25, 26, 29, 32)

23. Verbalize an understanding that bed rest and inactivity are seldom helpful for this condition and report the benefits of increased activity on feelings of well-being, improved mood, and increased self-esteem. (10, 33)

24. Verbalize adaptive philosophic and spiritual attitudes (e.g., benign does not mean imaginary, physical discomfort does not always have to be accompanied by emotional suffering). (6, 19, 34)

25. Verbalize a reduction in preoccupation with somatic concerns. (25, 35)

—. _____
   _____

—. _____
   _____

—. _____
   _____

20. Encourage the patient to consider the links between inactivity and depression.

21. Facilitate talk about concepts such as fairness, justice, and "pain" of living.

22. Help the patient to recognize and modify emotional response patterns and behaviors (e.g., unresolved grief, cue-generated panic, anger over past abuse) that may be rooted in past experiences and are being reactivated and magnified by fibromyalgia symptoms.

23. Teach the patient how negative cognitive distortions can readily lead to feelings of helplessness and anger.

24. Assist the patient in identifying distorted cognitive self-talk that fosters depression or anxiety.

25. Teach and reinforce positive, realistic cognitive self-talk as a means of coping with pain and depression.

26. Explore with the patient any past or current history of physical, sexual, or emotional abuse.

27. Instruct patient in anger management training (e.g., practicing forgiveness and tolerance, being assertive versus aggressive, delayed responding).

28. Train the patient to use cognitive techniques such as focused attention and visualization as tools in acquir-

ing psychophysiological self-regulation skills.

29. Teach the patient how to acquire relaxation through the use of breath control, muscle relaxation, and hand/foot warming.

30. Provide the patient with cassette tapes and written material for home practice of self-regulation skills.

31. Teach the patient how to move from self-relaxation to self-induced analgesia via a deeper application of cognitive and somatic self-regulation skills.

32. Assist the patient in recognizing sources of environmental stress and in reducing those that can be changed.

33. Reinforce the patient's reports of activity versus inactivity as the primary coping mechanism for pain, low energy, and depression.

34. Reinforce attitudes that reflect separation of physical discomfort from emotional distress.

35. Direct the patient to reserve a specific time each day (e.g., 15 to 30 minutes) to think about, discuss, and/or write about physical symptoms, while giving no time during the rest of the day to such activity.

___· _____
      _____
___· _____
      _____
___· _____
      _____

DIAGNOSTIC SUGGESTIONS

Axis I: 307.89   Pain Disorder Associated with Both
                       Psychological Factors and Fibromyalgia
              307.80   Pain Disorder Associated with Psychological
                       Factors
              316   Psychological Factors Affecting Fibromyalgia
              300.81   Somatization Disorder
              309.28   Adjustment Disorder with Mixed Anxiety and
                       Depressed Mood
              780.xx   Sleep Disorder Due to Fibromyalgia
              780.59   Sleep Disorder, Mixed Type
              _____   _____
              _____   _____

Axis II: 301.6   Dependent Personality Disorder
              301.4   Obsessive-Compulsive Personality Disorder
              _____   _____
              _____   _____

GYNECOLOGICAL AND OBSTETRIC CONDITIONS

BEHAVIORAL DEFINITIONS

1. Failure to appropriately care for self or developing fetus during pregnancy (e.g., abuse of alcohol or illicit drugs, poor eating habits, lack of compliance with medical recommendations, failure to regularly attend obstetric appointments).
2. Depressive symptomatology following childbirth that significantly impacts daily functioning and ability to care for newborn child.
3. Fertility problems that result in unresolved grief, depression, anger, or guilt.
4. Anxiety or depression associated with fertility assessment and treatment procedures.
5. Emotional distress and adjustment difficulties associated with menopause.

—. _____

_____

—. _____

_____

—. _____

_____

LONG-TERM GOALS

1. Implement coping strategies to enhance emotional adaptation to life changes and ongoing stressors.
2. Achieve and maintain compliance with prenatal medical care.
3. Give birth to a healthy infant.
4. Increase knowledge about pregnancy, childbirth, and childcare.

5. Address stressors, life changes, and marital conflict that are contributing to postpartum depression.
6. Resolve emotional distress associated with fertility problems.
7. Increase knowledge about available fertility treatments and come to decision with partner about which treatments and options to pursue.
8. Enhance adjustment to stressors associated with menopause.
9. Implement positive health behaviors (e.g., exercise, proper diet, regular sleep-wake cycle, abstinence from drugs and alcohol) to enhance physical and mental health.

—. _____

  _____

—. _____

  _____

—. _____

  _____

SHORT-TERM OBJECTIVES

1. Increase knowledge and sense of self-efficacy in coping with challenges of pregnancy, childbirth, and parenting. (1, 2)

2. Maintain compliance with recommended medical care for self and child. (3, 4)

3. Verbally express emotions associated with life changes caused by childbirth and caring for newborn. (5, 6, 11, 14)

4. Implement coping strategies and lifestyle changes to reduce tension, depression, anger, or frustration associated with stressors of new motherhood. (7, 8, 9, 12)

THERAPEUTIC INTERVENTIONS

1. Explore patient's fears and concerns about her parenting skills.

2. Help patient obtain information about pregnancy, childbirth, and care of her infant from sources such as medical professionals, books, and pamphlets.

3. Monitor and reinforce patient's compliance with recommended medical care during pregnancy and after childbirth.

4. Explore and address factors that interfere with patient's compliance with medical treatment, including faulty beliefs, educational or cog-

5. Identify and utilize sources of social support to provide assistance in caring for child and to allow time for rest and other activities. (8, 9, 10, 12)

6. Improve communication, reduce conflict, and enhance ability to assertively express desires and needs with significant other. (10, 11, 12, 13, 14)

7. Make positive statements about self and future that reflect improvements in self-esteem and optimism. (15)

8. Identify unrealistic expectations about motherhood and increase verbal acceptance of ambivalent feelings. (16)

9. Provide appropriate care for child, utilizing support system as needed. (9, 17)

10. Verbalize increased knowledge and understanding about postpartum depression. (18)

11. Share with therapist any suicidal or homicidal urges. (19)

12. Report no longer having thoughts of harming self or others. (19)

13. Verbally express grief, depression, anxiety, anger, or guilt associated with infertility and its treatment. (20, 26, 28)

14. Improve communication and reduce marital distress

nitive limitations, fears, or financial constraints.

5. Review stressors associated with caring for newborn infant (e.g., disruption in routine, sleep deprivation, decreased independence, social isolation, vocational changes).

6. Explore patient's emotional reactions to childcare-related stressors and normalize feelings of depression, frustration, and anxiety.

7. Assess amount of sleep, rest, and nutrition the patient and her infant are receiving.

8. Help patient identify ways to increase sleep and relaxation by modifying her schedule and utilizing sources of assistance and support in caring for infant.

9. Ask patient to identify sources of support and encourage her to utilize support system to help with care of infant.

10. Meet with patient and her partner to explore expectations and perceptions about sharing childcare responsibilities. Assist with communication and clarification if expectations are incompatible.

11. Explore and address patient's feelings of resentment, anger, guilt, or

associated with infertility. (21, 22)

15. Verbalize increased knowledge about infertility, treatment procedures, and other options. (23, 24, 27)

16. Agree with partner on a course of fertility treatment that both feel comfortable pursuing. (22, 24, 25, 26, 27)

17. Attend a support group for couples with fertility problems and process emotional reactions with therapist. (28)

18. Verbalize increased knowledge about menopause, associated physical changes, and available medical options. (29, 30, 31)

19. Identify current stressors, concerns, losses, and phase-of-life changes that are contributing to depression, anxiety, grief, frustration, or anger. (32, 33)

20. Develop and implement lifestyle changes, coping strategies, and increased self-acceptance to cope with phase-of-life stressors. (13, 34, 35, 36)

21. Discuss with therapist disruption in sexual functioning and identify potential contributing factors. (37)

22. Take antidepressant medication as prescribed and report any problems or side effects to therapist or physician. (38, 39, 40)

helplessness associated with implicit expectations that she take on the majority of childcare tasks without relinquishing other roles and obligations.

12. Assist patient and her significant other in developing strategies to provide more equitable distribution of childcare and household responsibilities as needed.

13. Use modeling, role playing, and behavioral rehearsal to teach assertiveness skills to enhance effective communication of needs and concerns with partner, family, friends, colleagues, and health care professionals.

14. Assess quality of marital relationship and current level of marital distress. Refer for or provide couples counseling if indicated.

15. Explore changes associated with childbirth that are affecting patient's self-esteem (e.g., body image issues, weight gain, loss of independence, marital changes, change in career status) and discuss options for addressing these concerns.

16. Examine patient's unrealistic expectations about motherhood (e.g., expectations of complete joy and happiness) and help her acknowledge and accept feelings of ambivalence.

23. Engage in a regular exercise routine. (41)

24. Maintain a healthy diet, including appropriate intake of vegetables, fruits, carbohydrates, and proteins, with decreased intake of fat, cholesterol, caffeine, salt, and sugar. (42)

25. Develop routines to maximize sleep and rest and to maintain an appropriate sleep-wake cycle. (43, 44)

26. Terminate abuse of alcohol and illicit drugs. (45, 46)

27. Terminate use or abuse of nicotine. (45, 47)

28. Share and process emotions about life changes and current concerns at a women's support group. (48)

—. _____
_____

—. _____
_____

—. _____
_____

17. Meet with partner and/or family members to discuss plan for childcare if patient is too depressed to care for baby appropriately.

18. Educate patient and significant other about postpartum blues and postpartum depression.

19. Assess patient for suicidal and homicidal ideation and arrange for psychiatric hospitalization if she is a danger to self or others.

20. Assess emotional impact on patient of fertility problems (e.g., grief, depression, anger, guilt) and encourage expression of emotions and concerns.

21. Explore impact of infertility on patient's relationship with significant other.

22. Provide couples counseling to address communication difficulties, disagreements, and marital distress surrounding fertility problems and treatment of infertility.

23. Explore patient's expectations and beliefs about fertility treatment and assess degree to which they are realistic.

24. Help patient obtain information about success rates and risks associated with fertility treatments.

25. If patient is considering in vitro fertilization, explore social, cultural, religious, and moral beliefs of patient

and partner that may impact their reactions to this procedure.

26. Encourage patient to discuss fears, anxieties, and concerns associated with fertility treatment.

27. Assist patient in exploring options (e.g., adoption) if fertility treatments are unsuccessful.

28. Refer patient and partner to a support group for couples with fertility problems.

29. Educate menopausal patient about normal changes associated with menopause (e.g., vasomotor flushes, vaginal dryness, genital atrophy, night sweats).

30. Refer patient to a medical doctor to assess need for hormone replacement therapy.

31. Help patient obtain information about risks and benefits of hormone replacement therapy.

32. Assist patient in identifying sources of daily stress.

33. Explore patient stressors, concerns, and losses that are contributing to emotional distress associated with menopause (e.g., negative expectations of menopause; death or illness of spouse or parent; changes in family, social, or work situation; fears of aging; health concerns; changes in physical appearance due to aging; family conflict).

34. Encourage and reinforce ongoing implementation of life changes that will reduce stress.

35. Teach patient coping strategies (e.g., problem solving, time management, assertiveness, communication skills) to manage daily stressors.

36. Encourage patient's expression of depression, grief, anger, or anxiety associated with stressors and losses.

37. Explore changes in patient's sexual activity and identify and address potential contributing factors (e.g., decreased sexual desire, depression, dyspareunia, decreased vaginal secretions, body image concerns).

38. Refer patient to a psychiatrist to assess possible need for antidepressant medication.

39. Monitor patient's compliance with antidepressant medication and encourage her to report side effects or problems to physician.

40. If patient is breast-feeding her child and in need of antidepressant medication, refer her to a physician who is familiar with the impact of antidepressants on breast-feeding and who can provide routine screenings of mother and infant to assess blood levels of medication.

41. Encourage patient to engage in regular aerobic exercise to enhance physical health. Use goal-setting and behavioral contracting to increase compliance. Explore options for adjusting schedule to increase time available for exercise.

42. Refer patient to a nutritionist or recommend a book on nutrition to educate her about healthy eating habits.

43. Encourage patient to maintain a regular sleep-wake cycle.

44. Explore and address factors that are interfering with appropriate sleep patterns (e.g., depression, caffeine use, stress, poor sleep habits) and educate patient about proper sleep hygiene.

45. Educate patient about the effects of drugs, alcohol, and nicotine on her health and, if applicable, on the developing fetus.

46. Assess patient for abuse of alcohol, illicit drugs, or prescription medications and refer her for treatment of chemical dependence if necessary.

47. Implement strategies to enhance patient's motivation to quit smoking and refer for or provide smoking cessation treatment. (See Cigarette Smoking chapter in this *Planner.*)

48. Refer patient to a women's support or focus group.

___. _____
    _____

___. _____
    _____

___. _____
    _____

DIAGNOSTIC SUGGESTIONS

Axis I:	296.2x	Major Depressive Disorder, Single Episode
	296.3x	Major Depressive Disorder, Recurrent
	311	Depressive Disorder, NOS
	309.0	Adjustment Disorder with Depressed Mood
	309.24	Adjustment Disorder with Anxiety
	309.28	Adjustment Disorder with Mixed Anxiety and Depressed Mood
	316	Psychological Factors Affecting (Axis III Disorder)
	V61.1	Partner Relational Problem
	V62.89	Phase of Life Problem
	V15.81	Noncompliance with Treatment
	_____	_____
	_____	_____

HEADACHE

BEHAVIORAL DEFINITIONS

1. Persistent head pain not related to significant structural changes such as tumors, strokes, aneurysms, CBS pressure, or infections.
2. Headache symptoms that interfere with ongoing daily activities and restrict quality of life.
3. Head pain that leads to excessive worry about its causes and treatments.
4. Worry about headaches that causes hesitancy to plan future activities.
5. Head pain that leads to overuse of and preoccupation with medications, often leading to strained relationships with physicians.
6. Head pain that is linked with feelings of depression, frustration, hopelessness, and helplessness.
7. Headaches that are accompanied by disruptive cognitive symptoms (e.g., light-headedness, confusion, inability to focus attention and concentration).
8. Headaches that are accompanied by unpleasant sensory and somatic symptoms (e.g., light and sound hypersensitivity, nausea and vomiting, fatigue and weakness).

__. _____
   _____

__. _____
   _____

__. _____
   _____

LONG-TERM GOALS

1. Reduce headache discomfort with greater reliance on behavioral management techniques and less dependence on painkilling medications.
2. Develop effective psychophysiologic self-regulation skills.
3. Maintain control of headaches with as little medication as possible.
4. Reduce disruption of daily activities caused by headache.
5. Eliminate dependence on medications that may be causing "rebound" headaches.
6. Increase awareness of mind/body interactions.
7. Develop strategies for dealing with internal and external sources of stress.
8. Reduce feelings of depression, anxiety, frustration, and desperation.
9. Resolve key life conflicts that may contribute to headaches.
10. Eliminate fear of "uncontrollable" headache emergencies.

__. _____

_____

__. _____

_____

__. _____

_____

SHORT-TERM OBJECTIVES	THERAPEUTIC INTERVENTIONS
1. Submit to a thorough physical exam to evaluate causes for and treatment of headache pain. (1)	1. Assist patient in finding a physician who can screen for nonbenign medical conditions and, if needed, work out a medication management plan.
2. Verbalize confidence in the medical diagnostic workup and a plan for medication management. (1, 2, 3, 5, 6, 8)	2. Review medical evaluation with patient and point out role of behavioral headache management alongside of medication use.
3. Use medication as prescribed and report benefits and problems to therapists and doctors. (1, 3, 5, 6, 8)	

4. Verbalize beliefs about causes for and effective control of headache pain. (4)

5. Verbalize a willingness and desire to implement behavioral headache-management techniques. (2, 5)

6. Eliminate most emergent behavior (e.g., ER visits, using other's medication, calling early for prescription refills). (1, 4, 5, 6)

7. Report a decrease in fear of being overwhelmed by headache pain. (1, 5, 7)

8. Recognize the problem of medication "rebound" headaches. (8)

9. Enhance understanding of the different types of and the many interactive causes for headaches. (5, 8, 9, 10)

10. Identify and avoid possible headache triggers. (10)

11. Verbalize an understanding of the risks and benefits, and rationale for and limitations of medication management strategies for headaches. (1, 6, 8, 11)

12. Verbalize an understanding of the complex role of stress in relation to headaches. (9, 12, 13)

13. Modify lifestyle to reduce stressors that can possibly be avoided. (12)

14. Verbalize an awareness of the distinction between stressors, mediating self-talk, and the emotional

3. Monitor medication as to effectiveness and/or side effects.

4. Assess patient's core beliefs about causes and control of headaches.

5. Provide patient with an overview of and a rationale for behavioral headache management that can reduce dependence on medication to control pain and increase functionality.

6. Discuss shortcomings of ER treatment of headaches (e.g., no long-term management plan, unknown doctor) and risks and limitations (e.g., increased tolerance, development of dependence, temptation for abuse) of opioid analgesics in treating pain of persistent headaches.

7. Assist patient in developing confidence-building self-talk (e.g., I can manage this pain, I am learning more effective coping skills, relief is on its way) that will reduce fear response to headache pain.

8. Explain meaning of "rebound" headaches as that term applies to overuse of medication.

9. Explain meaning of "rebound" headaches as that term applies to headaches that begin after interval of stress has ended.

and psychophysiological responses to stress. (12, 13, 14, 15)

15. Identify the distorted, tension-increasing, pain-exacerbating self-talk that is practiced in response to daily stressors. (13, 14, 15)

16. Implement positive, realistic self-talk in response to stressors that leads to a more calm, relaxed, confident attitude. (14, 15, 16, 17)

17. Acquire skill in psychophysiologic self-regulation and then implement it. (17, 18, 19, 20, 21)

18. Practice deep-muscle relaxation as a means of pain management. (18, 19, 20)

19. Utilize practical comfort aids without resorting to impatience, tension, and panic while letting headache run its natural course. (17, 21)

20. Accurately self-monitor headaches and medication use. (22)

21. Identify negative emotion response patterns that may contribute to or result from headache pain. (13, 23)

22. Implement positive health-related behaviors that may reduce headache pain and increase coping ability. (24)

10. Teach patient the role of triggers (e.g., foods, drinks, aromas) in headache pain and assist in identifying those that may be applicable. Provide a list of possible triggers for monitoring effects.

11. Teach the patient that medication management of headache pain has risks (e.g., physiological and/or psychological dependence, increased tolerance) and limitations (e.g., causes loss of alertness, restricts some activities, can be costly, has side effects) Explain the realistic role of medication and its rationale.

12. Assist patient in recognizing sources of environmental stress and in reducing those that can be changed.

13. Teach ways to recognize and modify emotional response patterns and behaviors (e.g., excessive perfectionism, anger) that may contribute to headaches.

14. Teach patient how negative, distorted cognitions (e.g., overgeneralization, catastrophizing, all-or-none thinking) can mediate a dysfunctional emotional, behavioral, and/or physiological response to a stressor. Mediating negative self-talk can exaggerate a stressor's impact, triggering more tension and pain.

—. _____
    _____
—. _____
    _____
—. _____
    _____

15. Assist patient in identifying the distorted schema and related automatic thoughts that mediate muscle tension, anxiety, and increased pain.

16. Teach and reinforce positive realistic, cognitive, self-talk as a means of coping with stressors more effectively.

17. Aid patient in understanding the integration of a cognitive-behavioral headache-management plan with appropriate medication use.

18. Train patient in use of psychophysiologic self-relaxation techniques (i.e., focused attention, mental imagery, muscle relaxation, sensory alteration).

19. Administer biofeedback to help patient identify signs of tension and learn deep-muscle relaxation.

20. Recommend to patient books on relaxation techniques (e.g., *The Relaxation Response* by Benson or *The Relaxation and Stress Reduction Workbook* by Davis, Eshelman, and McKay) and cassette tapes on Jacobsen's deep-muscle relaxation and the use of positive imagery.

21. Help patient to learn practical comfort aids (e.g., ice pack, avoid bright light) and avoid "catastrophizing" while waiting for a headache to run its natural course.

22. Teach the patient to maintain self-monitoring records and use them to spot trends and subtle changes in headache pattern.

23. Treat coexisting depression (see Depression chapter in this *Planner*) and/or anxiety (see Anxiety chapter in this *Planner*) where it has become intimate part of patient's headache pattern.

24. Help patient identify and modify as necessary such health-related behaviors as diet, exercise, and substance use.

—. _____
   _____

—. _____
   _____

—. _____
   _____

DIAGNOSTIC SUGGESTIONS

Axis I:	307.89	Pain Disorder Associated with Both Psychological Factors and (Axis III Disorder)
	307.80	Pain Disorder Associated with Psychological Factors
	300.81	Somatization Disorder
	304.80	Polysubstance Dependence
	304.10	Sedative, Hypnotic, or Anxiolytic Dependence
	316	Personality Traits Affecting (Axis III Disorder)
	316	Maladaptive Health Behaviors Affecting (Axis III Disorder)
	316	Psychological Symptoms Affecting (Axis III Disorder)
	_____	_____
	_____	_____

HIV/AIDS

BEHAVIORAL DEFINITIONS

1. A positive test for human immunodeficiency virus (HIV).
2. Decreased immune functioning (e.g., decreased numbers of T-helper lymphocyte cells) secondary to HIV infection.
3. Physical symptoms such as chronic low-grade fever, persistent fatigue, diarrhea, unintentional weight loss, skin rash, and night sweats.
4. Diagnosis of acquired immune deficiency syndrome (AIDS).
5. Development of AIDS-related illnesses (e.g., Kaposi's sarcoma, *Pneumocystis carinii* pneumonia, lymphoma, opportunistic infections, neurological disease).
6. Unresolved grief, anger, fear, or hopelessness associated with diagnosis of HIV or AIDS.
7. Emotional distress due to decline in physical health associated with HIV or AIDS.
8. Lack of compliance with medical treatment regimen.
9. Continued high-risk behaviors for transmitting HIV despite knowledge of HIV-positive status.
10. Coping difficulties associated with disease-related stressors (e.g., vocational changes, financial difficulties, loss of important relationships).

—. _____
  _____

—. _____
  _____

—. _____
  _____

LONG-TERM GOALS

1. Increase knowledge about HIV/AIDS and medical treatment options.
2. Decrease feelings of depression, fear, anxiety, and hopelessness.
3. Improve ability to identify, cope with, and appropriately express emotions associated with HIV diagnosis.
4. Improve quality of life and reduce disruption in daily activities caused by decline in physical health.
5. Develop positive attitudes and behaviors that promote feelings of peace, confidence, and acceptance in coping with HIV/AIDS and corresponding challenges and life changes.
6. Accept and maintain compliance with medical treatment regimen.
7. Acquire stress-management skills to enhance immune functioning and emotional adaptation to disease.
8. Develop adaptive coping skills for addressing stressors and losses associated with HIV infection.
9. Eliminate high-risk behaviors (e.g., intravenous drug use with unsterilized needles, unprotected sex) for transmitting HIV.
10. Improve communication with family, friends, and partners about disease and associated emotions.

__. _____
_____
__. _____
_____
__. _____
_____

SHORT-TERM OBJECTIVES	THERAPEUTIC INTERVENTIONS
1. Describe medical condition, treatment regimen, and prognosis as much as they are understood. (1)	1. Explore patient's understanding of HIV status, disease stage, and treatment options, while also assessing level of denial.
2. Verbalize increased knowledge about HIV and AIDS and treatment options. (2, 3)	2. Assist patient in acquiring information about HIV and AIDS from physicians, HIV/AIDS hotlines, the

3. Decrease level of verbal denial about HIV status, while increasing verbal acceptance. (1, 2, 4, 5, 23)

4. Comply with medication treatment regimen and necessary medical procedures. (6, 7, 8, 9)

5. Report to physicians any side effects or problems associated with medical treatment. (9)

6. Report to physicians or therapists any physical symptoms that cause concern. (10, 11, 12)

7. Increase assertiveness in interacting with health care professionals to gain a greater sense of control in managing medical condition. (11, 12, 13)

8. Implement positive dietary changes, such as maintaining adequate levels of nutrition, decreasing intake of fat and salt, and increasing intake of healthful foods. (14)

9. Terminate the use or abuse of drugs, alcohol, and/or nicotine. (15, 16)

10. Verbally express feelings of anxiety or depression associated with medical condition. (17, 23)

11. Verbalize increased knowledge about high-risk behaviors for transmitting or contracting HIV. (2, 18, 19)

American Foundation for AIDS Research, books, and reputable Internet sites.

3. Consult with patient's physician and other pertinent medical personnel to enhance coordination of medical and psychological treatments.

4. Confront patient's denial about the seriousness of condition and about the need to comply with medical treatment regimen.

5. Encourage realistic optimism versus denial to increase appropriate help-seeking and proactive health decisions.

6. Monitor and reinforce patient's compliance with medical treatment regimen.

7. Explore and address attitudes, misconceptions, and situational factors that interfere with patient's compliance with medical treatment regimen.

8. Assist patient in developing strategies to enhance adherence to medication regimen (e.g., self-monitoring of medication use, use of medication containers with preloaded pill compartments, prompts from significant others, reminder beepers).

9. Help patient develop mechanisms to ensure regular contact with medical personnel to address questions

12. Eliminate behaviors that are high risk for transmitting HIV to others, such as unprotected sexual contact and intravenous drug use with shared needles. (19, 20, 21)

13. Verbalize any thoughts of self-harm. (22)

14. Attend an HIV/AIDS support group and discuss impact of attending with therapist. (23)

15. Maintain a pattern of exercise (as recommended by physician) and a regular sleep/wake cycle. (24)

16. Report to therapist any observed changes in memory, concentration, and thinking. (25)

17. Develop a plan for coping with changes in cognitive functioning. (26)

18. Verbalize an understanding of the impact of stress on immune functioning. (27)

19. Identify and appropriately express needs, concerns, and emotions in verbal communications with therapist, family, and friends. (12, 13, 28)

20. Make a commitment to maintain a fighting spirit determined to overcome the physical and emotional challenges of HIV/AIDS. (29)

21. Identify life circumstances (e.g., vocational, financial, legal, interpersonal) that

regarding medication use and side effects.

10. Assist patient in monitoring physical symptoms that require medical attention and review the necessary steps for obtaining appropriate medical care.

11. Encourage patient to take an active role in medical treatment decision making.

12. Encourage and reinforce patient's assertiveness in asking questions, seeking information, expressing needs and disease-related symptoms, and sharing feelings.

13. Use modeling, role playing, and behavioral rehearsal to teach assertiveness skills, or refer patient for assertiveness training.

14. Refer patient to nutritionist or dietician to help prevent undue weight loss and/or vitamin and mineral deficiencies.

15. Assist patient in implementing smoking cessation strategies (see Cigarette Smoking chapter in this *Planner*) or refer for treatment of nicotine addiction.

16. Assess patient for substance abuse or dependence, and if necessary, refer for substance-abuse treatment. (See Chemical Dependence chapter in this *Planner*.)

17. Identify and treat coexisting depression and anxiety. (See

lead to stress, tension, or worry. (30, 32)

22. Implement changes in life situation to reduce level of stress. (31, 33)

23. Identify stressful situations that cannot be changed but must be coped with more effectively. (32)

24. Utilize relaxation or meditation techniques to reduce stress. (33)

25. Replace negative cognitions with more realistic, positive self-talk that reduces negative affect and promotes an optimistic outlook. (34, 35)

26. Develop a plan to increase the experience of humor and levity. (36)

27. Identify positive sources of social support. (37)

28. Utilize support system to implement lifestyle changes and to enhance coping with disease-related stressors. (23, 38)

29. Develop a plan for managing future deterioration in physical health (i.e., with respect to finances, treatment decisions, and identifying individuals to assist with caregiving). (39)

30. Express feelings of grief, loss, and fear associated with disease. (17, 40, 41, 42, 43)

31. Implement strategies for improving communication and quality of relationships with significant others. (44, 45)

Depression and Anxiety chapters in this *Planner.*)

18. Assess patient's level of knowledge about high-risk behaviors for contracting or transmitting HIV.

19. Educate patient or assist him/her in obtaining information about high-risk behaviors for HIV transmission (e.g., unprotected sexual contact, injection drug use with unsterile needles).

20. Emphasize to patient the importance of eliminating high-risk behaviors to avoid transmitting disease to others.

21. Monitor and reinforce patient's elimination of high-risk behaviors.

22. Assess patient for suicidal ideation, and arrange for hospitalization as necessary when he/she is judged to be a threat to self.

23. Refer patient to an HIV/AIDS support group and process reactions to attending the group.

24. Encourage patient to follow exercise regimen, as medically indicated, as well as regular sleeping patterns.

25. Monitor deficits in patient's cognitive functioning and if needed refer to appropriate health care professionals (e.g., neurologist and/or neuropsychologist) to assess for HIV-related dementia or other neurological disorders.

32. Inform previous partners and current significant others about HIV status. (46)

33. Identify life priorities, goals, and aspirations, and develop a specific plan for implementing them. (47, 48)

34. Identify enjoyable activities and incorporate them into daily life. (49)

35. Express feelings of shame, low self-esteem, and fears of rejection associated with HIV status. (50)

36. Report a decrease in feelings of shame and negative self-evaluation. (51, 52)

__. _____
   _____

__. _____
   _____

__. _____
   _____

26. Assist patient in developing strategies to compensate for cognitive deficits (e.g., use of reminders such as lists and calendars, breaking difficult tasks down into smaller steps).

27. Educate patient about the physiological effects of stress on immune system functioning.

28. Encourage and reinforce patient's expression of needs and emotions with therapist and significant others.

29. Challenge patient to maintain a positive attitude in order to create a physiological, emotional, and spiritual environment that will help fight disease and maximize healing powers. Recommend reading *You Can Fight for Your Life* (LeShan) and/or *Anatomy of an Illness* (Cousins).

30. Assist patient in identifying current stressors and in distinguishing between controllable and uncontrollable aspects of stressful situations.

31. Assist patient in the development of active coping skills (e.g., assertiveness, problem solving, modifying life circumstances, improved communication skills) to address vocational, relational, financial, and legal stressors.

32. Help patient identify stressors that cannot be altered and that require acceptance and more effective coping strategies.

33. Train patient in the use of relaxation, visualization, and/or meditation techniques to manage stress and create a more peaceful frame of mind.

34. Teach patient to identify negative, distorted cognitions and automatic thoughts in response to stressors.

35. Teach patient to replace negatively biased thoughts with more positive, realistic self-talk.

36. Assign patient to read a humorous book or to watch a funny movie and report the effects of this experience on attitude and mood.

37. Ask patient to identify existing sources of social support.

38. Encourage involvement of patient's support network in treatment planning, adherence to treatment regimen, and implementation of lifestyle changes.

39. Assist patient in anticipating and developing an action plan for future declines in physical health.

40. Explore and process patient's fears associated with deterioration of physical health, dying, and death.

41. Assign patient to keep a daily journal of emotions. Process journal entries in therapy sessions.

42. Assist patient in appropriately grieving losses associated with illness (e.g., decline in physical health, loss of vocational status, relationship changes).

43. Explore and process patient's emotions associated with HIV diagnosis and current stage of disease.

44. Explore with patient the impact of disease on relationships with significant others. Help patient develop strategies for enhancing communication with others about HIV/AIDS.

45. Refer patient for family or couples therapy to address interpersonal conflict or communication problems.

46. Help patient develop a plan for disclosing HIV status to others (e.g., friends, family members, and past sexual partners) and process emotions associated with this.

47. Assign patient to make a list of unfinished tasks and life priorities. Assist patient in developing a plan for completing important tasks and priorities.

48. Explore patient's hopes and goals for the future and help him/her develop strategies for reaching these goals.

49. Assist patient in developing rewarding and enjoyable daily activities to increase life satisfaction.

50. Explore and process patient's feelings of shame and stigma associated with HIV status.

51. Assign patient to identify positive characteristics about self.

52. Verbally reinforce patient's positive statements of confidence, self-worth, and accomplishments.

__. _____
   _____

__. _____
   _____

__. _____
   _____

DIAGNOSTIC SUGGESTIONS

Axis I:	316	Psychological Factors Affecting HIV/AIDS
	309.0	Adjustment Disorder with Depressed Mood
	309.24	Adjustment Disorder with Anxiety
	309.28	Adjustment Disorder with Mixed Anxiety and Depressed Mood
	309.3	Adjustment Disorder with Disturbance of Conduct
	304.80	Polysubstance Dependence
	307.89	Pain Disorder Associated with Both Psychological Factors and HIV/AIDS
	V15.81	Noncompliance with Treatment
	_____	_____
	_____	_____

IRRITABLE BOWEL SYNDROME (IBS)

BEHAVIORAL DEFINITIONS

1. Crampy abdominal pain, gassiness, bloating, and changes in bowel habits (i.e., constipation or diarrhea or both in succession) in the absence of any organic disease to explain the symptoms.
2. Disruption of normal activities; fear of social events, going to work, or travel.
3. High stress and/or poor stress-coping skills often stimulate symptoms.
4. Anxiety, depression, and preoccupation with somatic concerns.
5. Frustration with treatment professionals because medical treatments produce disappointing results.

__. _____

_____

__. _____

_____

__. _____

_____

LONG-TERM GOALS

1. Reduce pain and other bowel symptoms.
2. Become as knowledgeable and self-reliant as possible in management of the condition.
3. Establish a trusting relationship with a doctor who is knowledgeable about IBS.
4. Develop eating habits and choice of foods that minimize symptoms while providing good nutrition.

5. Develop and practice ways of thinking that can reduce preoccupation with symptoms.
6. Develop and practice behavioral and psychophysiologic stress-management skills.
7. Minimize the impact of the symptoms on daily activities.

—. _____
   _____
—. _____
   _____
—. _____
   _____

SHORT-TERM OBJECTIVES

1. Describe history, treatment, and symptoms of IBS. (1)

2. Identify changes made in life as an accommodation to IBS. (2)

3. Verbalize an increased understanding of IBS symptoms and management. (3, 4, 5)

4. Verbalize confidence in treating physician. (6)

5. Make a commitment to be actively involved in symptom management through emotional and behavioral changes. (7, 8, 9)

6. Verbalize acceptance of the fact that regulating diet, reducing stress, and improving stress-management skills are key elements in controlling IBS. (7, 8, 9)

THERAPEUTIC INTERVENTIONS

1. Gather a history of patient's IBS, its treatment, and symptoms.

2. Explore the effect IBS has had on patient's life (i.e., behavior, attitudes, relationships, responsibilities, and feelings).

3. Assist patient in obtaining verbal and written information about IBS from sources such as health care professionals, reputable Internet sites, and bookstores.

4. Reassure patient that there is no evidence that IBS symptoms are likely to lead to more severe conditions like inflammatory bowel disease or cancer.

5. Teach the patient what benign "functional" bowel symptoms are.

7. Carefully self-monitor diet, stress, medications, and exercise to help identify what may trigger symptoms and what may minimize symptoms. (10)

8. Modify diet and use dietary supplements to improve bowel functioning. (11, 12)

9. Report the steps taken to maintain normal social and marital/family relationships. (13)

10. Increase the amount of daily physical exercise as a means of building physical strength, reducing stress, and improving mood. (14, 15)

11. Develop and implement a plan for termination of cigarette smoking. (16)

12. Limit the consumption of caffeine and alcohol to not more than one portion (i.e., one cup of coffee and one alcoholic beverage) per day. (17)

13. Utilize clothing aids to manage bowel symptoms and to allow for maintenance of normal life responsibilities. (18)

14. Reduce the level of reactivity to environmental stress by modifying stressors and/or by developing improved coping skills. (19, 22)

15. Identify automatic thoughts that can trigger anxiety and tension and increase IBS symptoms. (20, 21)

6. Discuss with patient his/her relationships with doctors. If necessary, recommend a physician who takes a positive approach to management of IBS.

7. Challenge beliefs and misinformation that encourage passivity and helplessness on patient's part.

8. Describe to patient potential dangers of overreliance on medication to control benign functional bowel symptoms.

9. Teach the patient that his/her behavior is crucial to managing IBS symptoms (i.e., careful regulation of diet and stress-management are the mainstays of symptom management).

10. Teach the patient to maintain self-monitoring records of food intake, exercise, stress level, and symptoms.

11. Provide the patient with information on foods and dietary supplements that can improve bowel functioning.

12. Refer patient to a dietician who can instruct him/her regarding the interaction between IBS and diet.

13. Encourage the patient to seek out and maintain normal social and sexual relationships rather than withdrawing because of IBS symptoms.

16. Increase the use of positive self-talk in response to IBS symptoms and other stressors. (22)

17. Identify past or current experiences of physical, sexual, or emotional abuse. (23)

18. Learn ways to direct thinking away from worry about IBS symptoms. (22, 24)

19. Learn and use psychophysiologic self-relaxation skills (i.e., slow-deep breathing, muscle relaxation, hand warming) to manage somatic reaction to stress. (25, 26, 27)

20. Practice and implement anal sphincter contraction to control fecal incontinence. (28)

21. Verbalize ways to reduce frustration and manage anger toward those who seem critical and unsupportive. (29)

22. Develop confidence in self-management of mild and moderate symptoms by trying diet and cognitive-behavioral techniques before calling doctor. (30)

__. _____

_____

__. _____

_____

__. _____

_____

14. Assist the patient in developing a routine of daily physical exercise.

15. Recommend that the patient read and implement programs from *Exercising Your Way to Better Mental Health* by Leith.

16. Assist the patient in developing and implementing a plan to stop smoking. (See Cigarette Smoking chapter in this *Planner.*)

17. Teach the patient the harmful effects of consuming large amounts of caffeine and/or alcohol, and solicit an agreement to limit intake to low levels.

18. Teach the patient practical measures, such as clothing aids, for managing embarrassing bowel symptoms.

19. Assist the patient in recognizing sources of environmental stress and in reducing or eliminating those stressors that can be changed.

20. Teach the patient how negative cognitive distortions can readily lead to feelings of anticipatory anxiety and anger that exacerbate IBS symptoms.

21. Assist the patient in identifying distorted cognitive self-talk that fosters anxiety and stress reactions.

22. Teach and reinforce positive, realistic cognitive self-talk as a means of coping with stressors and IBS symptoms.

23. Explore with the patient any past or current history of physical, sexual, or emotional abuse.

24. Develop a cognitive behavioral coping plan to counter the patient's excessive preoccupation with symptoms or related concerns such as location of bathrooms while away from home.

25. Train the patient to use cognitive techniques (such as focused attention and visualization) as tools in acquiring psychophysiological self-regulation skills.

26. Teach the patient how to acquire relaxation through the use of breath control, muscle relaxation, and hand/foot warming.

27. Provide the patient with cassette tapes and written material for home practice of self-regulation skills.

28. Provide patient with specialized biofeedback training for strengthening external anal sphincter contraction to aid in the control of fecal incontinence.

29. Instruct the patient in anger management (e.g., practicing forgiveness and tolerance, being assertive versus aggressive, delayed responding).

30. Encourage the patient to
    try self-management of
    symptoms without calling a
    doctor, unless symptoms
    suddenly become worse,
    there is continuous severe
    pain, a fever accompanies
    pain, or blood is visible in
    the stool.

__. _____
    _____

__. _____
    _____

__. _____
    _____

DIAGNOSTIC SUGGESTIONS

Axis I:
300.81	Somatization Disorder
307.89	Pain Disorder Associated with Both Psychological Factors and Irritable Bowel Syndrome
316	Stress-Related Physiological Response Affecting Irritable Bowel Syndrome
307.50	Eating Disorder NOS
787.6	Encopresis, with Constipation and Overflow Incontinence
_____	_____
_____	_____

MULTIPLE SCLEROSIS (MS)

BEHAVIORAL DEFINITIONS

1. Demyelination occurring simultaneously in many areas of the brain or spinal cord, leading to sensory and motor dysfunction.
2. High frustration and anxiety during the years between irregularly occurring, unexplained symptoms and a firm diagnosis of MS.
3. High uncertainty and worry regarding the future course of the disease.
4. Motor symptoms such as muscle fatigue, weakness, spasticity, stiffness, and loss of coordination.
5. Muscle control deterioration effects such as loss of balance, dizziness, loss of bladder and bowel control, and difficulty speaking.
6. Sensory symptoms such as pain, vision loss, numbness, and sensations of pins and needles.
7. Depression and anxiety secondary to the losses associated with the disease, lesions in emotional pathways in brain, and possibly from some of the drugs used to treat MS.
8. Family disruption caused by unpredictability of the disease, with potential for progression to severe and permanent disability.

—. _____

_____

—. _____

_____

—. _____

_____

LONG-TERM GOALS

1. Minimize the physical and emotional impact of MS as much as possible.
2. Become as knowledgeable as possible about MS, using all available resources to help with remaining as self-reliant as possible in dealing with the disease.
3. Make arrangements for the future that will help self and family adjust, if necessary, to the progressive deterioration of functioning.
4. Increase compliance with and adjustment to necessary medical procedures.
5. Understand and practice positive health behaviors.
6. Acquire stress- and pain-management skills to enhance coping with effects of the disease.

—. _____

_____

—. _____

_____

—. _____

_____

SHORT-TERM OBJECTIVES

1. Become as knowledgeable as possible regarding MS, and accurately verbalize information about the symptoms, regulation, and unpredictable course of this disease. (1, 2, 3)

2. Verbalize frustration and fears that were experienced during the lengthy period when symptoms were sporadic and diagnosis uncertain. (3, 4, 5)

3. Verbally express feelings of depression and anxiety about medical condition and

THERAPEUTIC INTERVENTIONS

1. Explore patient's understanding of MS, assisting in obtaining accurate information from sources such as health care professionals, books, and reputable Internet sites.

2. Challenge attitudes of both excessive denial and excessive fatalism regarding patient's MS.

3. Explore patient's history of symptom development and encourage him/her to talk about experiences leading to diagnosis.

possible long-term deterioration of health. (2, 4, 5)

4. Verbalize an emotionally balanced reaction to diagnosis—neither denial nor helpless fatalism. (2, 4, 5, 11)

5. Assertively ask clear questions of those involved in managing health, and verbalize concerns about direction and quality of medical care. (6, 7)

6. Establish a trusting relationship with a compassionate physician who is knowledgeable about all types of neurologic dysfunction. (8, 11)

7. Accept referral to a specialized MS treatment center if full range of psychosocial, educational, and rehabilitation needs are not being addressed by current care plan. (8, 9, 10)

8. Actively participate in rehabilitative activities that may help maintain or even restore some aspects of functioning. (9, 10)

9. Comply with medication regimen and necessary medical procedures, reporting any side effects to physicians. (8, 11, 12)

10. Carefully self-monitor conditions that may cause exacerbation of MS symptoms and report them to physicians and therapists. (13, 14)

4. Normalize patient's feelings of grief, sadness, and anxiety as part of the reaction to a diagnosis of MS, and encourage verbal expression of these emotions.

5. Empathize with and process patient's feelings regarding the high degree of uncertainty regarding the course of MS.

6. Use role playing, modeling, and behavior rehearsal to train the patient in assertiveness.

7. Role play and encourage the asking of clear questions of those involved in patient's medical care and support.

8. Consult with patient's physician and other pertinent medical personnel to enhance coordination of medical and psychological treatments.

9. Refer patient to specialized MS treatment center, if indicated, where a full range of medical, rehabilitation, educational, and psychosocial services is offered.

10. Help patient to understand and verbalize the adaptive value of rehabilitation, even within the context of a progressive disease.

11. Explore and address patient misconceptions, fears, and situational factors that interfere with compliance with medical treatment.

11. Verbalize a behavioral plan to cope with a hot environment and the potential elevation of body temperature. (14, 15)

12. Terminate smoking. (16)

13. Terminate the use of alcohol. (16)

14. Engage in a medically appropriate level of regular exercise and physical activity. (17, 18)

15. Verbalize an understanding of the fatigue element in planning activities and implement the skill of effectively pacing activity. (14, 18)

16. Maintain an active lifestyle to the extent possible, keeping up (with modifications as needed) past activities, skills, and interests to the degree possible. (19)

17. Implement a routine schedule of adequate rest and sleep. (20, 27)

18. Verbalize feelings related to changes in role functioning as parent, breadwinner, spouse, friend, etc. (21)

19. Self-monitor internal and external sources of stress and note a possible link between stress and exacerbation of MS symptoms. (22, 23)

20. Identify and reduce those sources of external stress that can reasonably be changed or avoided. (23)

12. Review with patient the available pain treatment options and their potential benefits and risks.

13. Assist patient in knowledgeably self-monitoring MS symptoms as well as any other medical symptoms that require medical attention.

14. Reinforce patient for monitoring and engaging in behaviors that promote general health. Remind him/her of conditions that increase risk of MS exacerbation (e.g., fever, infection, fatigue, rise in body temperature).

15. Discuss with patient the negative effects of elevated body temperature on MS symptoms and assist in developing a behavioral plan for coping with temperature.

16. Encourage patient to terminate smoking and alcohol consumption. (See Cigarette Smoking chapter in this *Planner*.)

17. Encourage patient to exercise regularly, and refer him/her to a physical or occupational therapist for exercise and activity guidance.

18. Aid patient in planning physical activities, taking into account the fact that the rapid onset of fatigue, to the point of partial loss of motor functioning, can be a part of the MS picture.

21. Verbalize significant life events that lead to depression, tension, or stress. (21, 22, 23, 24)

22. Identify distorted cognitions that occur in response to daily events and illness-related stressors and that contribute to anxiety or depression. (25)

23. Increase the use of positive self-talk in response to symptoms or other sources of stress. (26)

24. Acquire and implement the use of psychophysiological self-relaxation skills invoking breath control, muscle relaxation, and mental imagery. (27, 29)

25. Learn and use the cognitive self-analgesia strategy of focusing attention on pleasant distracting images and sensations that can inhibit discomfort. (28, 29)

26. Make appropriate use of personal, vocational, marital/family counseling as needed. (30)

27. Regularly attend a support group. (31)

28. Verbalize adaptive philosophic and spiritual attitudes toward disease, pain, and suffering. (31, 32)

29. Verbalize an attitude of hope, peace, and joy to help resist the disease process. (31, 32, 33)

19. Help patient remain focused on educational, vocational, social, and recreational interests as long as possible. Discourage him/her from allowing MS to become the primary focus of personal identity.

20. Teach patient the benefits of keeping a routine schedule of adequate sleeping hours and how to use behavioral and cognitive techniques (e.g., regular exercise, avoidance of naps, reduced stimulation at night, practicing of relaxation skills, use of positive imagery) to induce sleep.

21. Help patient with advanced MS deal with frustration resulting from his/her diminished role as breadwinner, spouse, friend, or parent.

22. Raise patient's awareness of mind-body relationships and point out possible effects of stress on MS exacerbation.

23. Aid patient in recognizing sources of environmental stress and in reducing those that can be modified.

24. Assess and treat patient depression and anxiety. (See Depression and Anxiety chapters in this *Planner.*)

25. Help patient to recognize dysfunctional patterns of thinking—distorted automatic thoughts and emotional responses that may

30. Communicate to family members facts and feelings regarding the progression of the disease. (33)

31. Attend family therapy sessions in which a plan is developed for how care will be handled if deterioration is progressive. (33, 34, 35)

32. Recognize the fact that nervous system lesions associated with MS can cause cognitive deficits in attention, memory, and reasoning as well as poor emotional control. (35)

33. Cooperate with a referral to neurologist and/or neuropsychologist to evaluate cognitive dysfunction. (36)

—. _____
   _____

—. _____
   _____

—. _____
   _____

contribute to high levels of stress.

26. Teach and reinforce positive, realistic cognitive self-talk as a way for patient to cope with internal and external stress.

27. Instruct patient in how to use cognitive and somatic self-relaxation techniques such as breath control, muscle relaxation, and visual imagery.

28. Teach patient how to move from self-relaxation to the use of imagery analgesia and affirmative coping imagery.

29. Provide patient with cassette tapes and written materials for home practice of self-regulation skills.

30. Encourage use of and make referrals as needed for personal, vocational, and marital/family counseling.

31. Encourage patient to participate regularly in an MS support group, if one is available.

32. Facilitate talk about philosophic and spiritual coping with feelings about life with MS, encouraging patient to rely on philosophic and spiritual faith resources that have been helpful in coping with past suffering.

33. In a family therapy session acknowledge with patient and family members that coping with MS can be diffi-

cult and that coping requires both external social support and internal emotional and spiritual fortitude. Encourage sharing of feelings between family members.

34. Help family members plan for future care needs that will arise if disease progresses.

35. Help family members understand that lesions in emotional centers of brain may cause uncontrollable laughing or crying that may not be under voluntary control.

36. Arrange for neurological and neuropsychological evaluation if patient demonstrates signs of cognitive dementia.

___. _____
    _____

___. _____
    _____

___. _____
    _____

DIAGNOSTIC SUGGESTIONS

Axis I: 316   Psychological Factors Affecting Multiple
                       Sclerosis Condition
           307.89   Pain Disorder Associated with Both
                       Psychological Factors and Multiple Sclerosis
           311   Depressive Disorder NOS
           294.1   Dementia Due to Multiple Sclerosis
           293.89   Anxiety Disorder Due to Multiple Sclerosis
           _____   _____
           _____   _____

OBESITY

BEHAVIORAL DEFINITIONS

1. Weighing more than 20 percent above one's ideal weight as indicated by actuarial height-weight tables.
2. An elevated body mass index (i.e., BMI greater than or equal to 27).
3. Waist-to-hip circumference ratio that exceeds 0.80 for women or 0.95 for men, indicating a large concentration of fat around the abdomen.
4. Medical complications or exacerbation of medical problems (e.g., cardiovascular disease, hypertension, diabetes) due to being overweight.
5. Overweight that is caused by poor eating habits (e.g., high intake of salt, fat, or excessive calories) or off-and-on ("yo-yo") dieting.
6. Episodes of binge eating, characterized by rapid consumption of large quantities of food in a short time and feelings of lack of control over eating that contribute to being overweight.

—. _____
   _____

—. _____
   _____

—. _____
   _____

LONG-TERM GOALS

1. Reduce weight and/or body fat to less than 20 percent over ideal weight.
2. Increase positive health behaviors, including healthy eating patterns and regular exercise.

3. Decrease unhealthy eating habits, such as binge eating, yo-yo dieting, and excessive intake of fat, cholesterol, and salt.
4. Reduce feelings of shame, inferiority, and low self-esteem associated with weight or body size.
5. Resolve life conflicts that may contribute to binge eating and other unhealthy eating patterns.

—. _____

_____

—. _____

_____

—. _____

_____

SHORT-TERM OBJECTIVES

1. Cooperate with a physical exam to assess possible medical causes for and consequences of obesity. (1)
2. Verbalize an understanding of appropriate nutrition and eating habits. (2, 3)
3. Plan meals and eat at set times (i.e., rather than self-deprivation followed by overeating). (3)
4. Improve eating habits, including decreasing intake of fat, salt, cholesterol, and calories, and increasing intake of healthful foods. (3, 4)
5. Set realistic goals for weight loss. (5)
6. Verbalize an understanding of the risks of yo-yo dieting and extreme dietary restrictions. (6, 17)

THERAPEUTIC INTERVENTIONS

1. Refer patient to a physician for a physical exam.
2. Refer patient to a nutritionist or dietician for nutritional counseling.
3. Educate patient regarding proper nutrition (i.e., decreasing fat, salt, and cholesterol intake, and increasing intake of healthful foods) and healthy eating habits (e.g., eating at set times).
4. Assist patient in meal planning.
5. Assist patient in setting appropriate, realistic goals for weight loss.
6. Explain to patient how yo-yo dieting and extreme dietary restraint are counterproductive (i.e., may contribute to increased health risks, decreased metabolic

7. Terminate problematic use of diet pills, laxatives, and diuretics. (7)

8. Accurately self-monitor eating patterns and mood and situational factors associated with eating by keeping a written daily record. (8, 9)

9. Identify food cues and possible triggers for overeating. (9, 10, 17)

10. Implement stimulus control and self-control techniques for overeating. (10, 11)

11. Implement alternative coping strategies for dealing with negative affect and situational stressors that trigger overeating. (12, 17, 19, 25)

12. List alternative activities to use in coping with eating triggers. (13)

13. Increase regular exercise and daily physical activity. (14, 15)

14. Attend a self-help support group that focuses on achieving and maintaining weight loss. (16)

15. Read educational material on eating disorders. (17)

16. Identify distorted, unrealistic self-talk that is practiced in response to daily stressors and that exacerbates negative affect or feelings of low self-esteem. (18)

17. Identify unrealistic expectations and distorted, irrational beliefs regarding body weight and shape. (19, 20, 21)

rate, and increased fat deposits) in achieving and maintaining weight loss.

7. Educate patient about the risks (e.g., fluid and electrolyte abnormalities) of excessive or inappropriate use of diet pills, laxatives, or diuretics.

8. Teach patient to maintain a diary of food intake, including type and amount of food consumed, plus thoughts, feelings, and situational factors associated with eating.

9. Process diary information to help identify food cues and triggers for overeating.

10. Teach patient to utilize stimulus control techniques (e.g., restrict eating to certain places, situations, and times of the day; limit availability of unhealthy foods).

11. Teach patient self-control techniques, such as slowing down eating, focusing on each bite, and setting down utensil between bites.

12. Assist patient in the development of coping strategies (e.g., problem solving, anger management, communication skills) to manage negative affect and interpersonal stressors that trigger overeating.

13. Assist patient in generating a list of alternative activities to utilize in response to eating triggers (e.g., taking

18. Implement positive, realistic self-talk with respect to weight and daily eating patterns. (19, 22)

19. Identify the role of family-of-origin issues in the development of unhealthy eating patterns. (23)

20. Identify and utilize sources of social support in facilitating and maintaining changes in eating patterns. (16, 24, 25)

21. Implement assertive behaviors to increase expression of feelings, getting needs met, and setting appropriate boundaries on eating behavior. (26)

22. Develop a plan for coping with overeating relapses and dieting setbacks. (12, 13, 27, 28)

23. Express feelings of shame, inferiority, and fear of rejection associated with obesity. (29)

24. Report a decrease in feelings of shame, inferiority, and/or fear of negative evaluation associated with weight. (30, 31)

—. _____
   _____

—. _____
   _____

—. _____
   _____

a walk, talking to a friend, listening to music, writing in a journal).

14. Assist patient in developing a plan to integrate regular exercise into daily schedule.

15. Reinforce increased daily physical activity by patient, such as walking or biking rather than driving, and using the stairs rather than the elevator.

16. Refer patient to a self-help or support group such as Overeaters Anonymous (OA) or TOPS.

17. Assign patient to read the book *Overcoming Binge Eating* by Fairburn or *Breaking Free from Compulsive Eating* by Ross.

18. Assist patient in identifying and modifying negative, distorted cognitions in response to interpersonal stressors.

19. Help patient to identify and modify maladaptive beliefs about dieting, weight, and body size.

20. Explore and challenge patient's prejudices, stereotypes, and preconceptions regarding obesity.

21. Explore the role of unrealistic, negative beliefs about body weight and size in maintaining patient's negative self-evaluation, social anxiety, and/or avoidance of social situations.

22. Teach patient realistic, positive self-talk as a more effective means of coping with stressors.

23. Explore and process the role of family-of-origin issues in patient's development and maintenance of unhealthy eating patterns.

24. Ask patient to identify existing sources of social support.

25. Discuss ways for patient to develop and maintain a positive support system.

26. Provide assertiveness training or refer patient to an assertiveness training class, emphasizing the need for setting boundaries on eating in social settings.

27. Educate patient about the relapse process and help identify high-risk situations and potential triggers for overeating, as well as alternative ways for coping effectively.

28. Educate patient on how to cope with setbacks by cognitively reframing lapses as mistakes that can be utilized to prompt restorative coping strategies (i.e., rather than viewing a lapse as a catastrophic failure that leads to continued overeating).

29. Explore patient's feelings of shame, inferiority, and fear of rejection that are associated with obesity.

30. Assist patient in identifying positive talents, traits, successes, and accomplishments that serve to build self-esteem and self-confidence.

31. Reinforce patient's statements of positive self-evaluation.

__. _____

_____

__. _____

_____

__. _____

_____

DIAGNOSTIC SUGGESTIONS

Axis I: 307.50   Eating Disorder NOS
307.51   Bulimia Nervosa
316   Maladaptive Health Behaviors Affecting (Axis III Disorder)
316   Personality Traits Affecting (Axis III Disorder)
316   Psychological Symptoms Affecting (Axis III Disorder)

_____   _____

_____   _____

ORGAN TRANSPLANTATION

BEHAVIORAL DEFINITIONS

1. Patient is a candidate for or a recipient of an organ transplantation.
2. Diagnosis of end-stage liver, kidney, heart, or lung disease.
3. Fear or worry about undergoing organ transplantation.
4. Unrealistic expectations about transplant surgery outcome.
5. Feelings of anxiety associated with prolonged wait for donor organ.
6. Anxiety, fear, and worry associated with physical symptoms (e.g., shortness of breath, cardiac symptoms) or required medical procedures.
7. Feelings of depression, helplessness, or hopelessness about decline in physical health and daily functioning.
8. Lack of compliance with medical treatment.
9. Stress associated with maintaining complex medical treatment regimen and required lifestyle changes after transplant.
10. Continued unhealthy behaviors (e.g., smoking, poor diet, substance abuse, inactivity) despite physician's recommendation to alter these behaviors.

__. _____
   _____

__. _____
   _____

__. _____
   _____

LONG-TERM GOALS

1. Increase knowledge about organ transplantation process and aftercare.

2. Enhance ability to effectively cope with all stages of the transplant process, including assessment of suitability for transplant, waiting for donor organ, transplant surgery, rehabilitation, and long-term aftercare.
3. Decrease anxiety, fear, or worry associated with medical condition and transplant procedure.
4. Reduce feelings of depression or hopelessness.
5. Increase sense of personal mastery in managing medical condition and associated stressors.
6. Improve quality of life and reduce disruption in daily activities caused by transplantation recovery process.
7. Achieve and maintain compliance with medical treatment regimen before and after transplant.
8. Implement and maintain healthy behaviors (e.g., proper diet and exercise, no nicotine or substance use) before and after transplant.
9. Develop positive attitudes and behaviors that promote feelings of peace, confidence, and acceptance in coping with medical illness and corresponding life changes.

—. _____
   _____
   _____
—. _____
   _____
   _____
—. _____
   _____

SHORT-TERM OBJECTIVES

1. Verbalize an understanding of transplant procedure, including risks, required lifestyle changes, aftercare, and prognosis. (1, 2, 3, 4)

2. Verbally express expectations, concerns, fears, and hopes about transplant procedure and its outcome. (1, 2)

3. Comply with medical treatment regimen, reporting

THERAPEUTIC INTERVENTIONS

1. Review patient's understanding of the transplant procedure, including risks, prognosis, and aftercare.

2. Explore patient's expectations about organ transplant surgery and surgical outcome, including significant concerns, fears, or unrealistic hopes.

3. Assist patient in clarifying any questions or mispercep-

any problems or side effects to appropriate health care professionals. (5, 6, 7)

4. Identify any barriers to compliance with medical recommendations. (8, 9)

5. Implement active coping strategies to enhance sense of control in managing medical condition and associated stressors. (10, 11, 38)

6. Identify support persons to assist with care before and after transplant. (12, 13, 14, 15)

7. Attend family therapy sessions focused on open communication regarding stressors associated with medical condition. (14, 15)

8. Develop a plan for moving to city where transplant center is located (if needed), including living and financial arrangements. (14, 15)

9. Report to therapist any psychological or psychiatric symptoms that interfere with functioning or cause concern. (16, 32)

10. Terminate the use or abuse of alcohol or illicit drugs. (17)

11. Terminate the use of nicotine. (18)

12. Verbally express emotions and concerns associated with waiting for and receiving donor organ. (19, 20, 21)

13. Seek information and support from other transplant

tions regarding transplant surgery with transplant team.

4. Consult with members of transplant team to communicate any psychosocial factors that may impact patient's suitability or readiness for transplant (e.g., poor compliance, substance abuse, severe psychiatric disorder) and to enhance coordination of medical and psychological interventions.

5. Assess patient's ability to understand medical instructions and care for self appropriately, identifying any cognitive, developmental, or emotional factors that may interfere.

6. Review patient's current medical treatment regimen, including consistency of and feelings about the use of medications, physical therapy, breathing treatments, nebulizers, bronchodilators, dialysis, etc.

7. Assess patient's history of compliance with medical treatment, as well as current compliance.

8. Monitor and reinforce patient's ongoing compliance with treatment regimen, using behavioral contracting, self-monitoring, and goal setting to enhance compliance.

9. Explore and address factors that may interfere with patient's compliance with

candidates and recipients. (22, 23)

14. Attend a support group for transplant candidates. (23)

15. Reach and maintain ideal body weight. (24)

16. Implement positive dietary changes such as increased intake of healthy foods and decreased intake of sodium, fat, cholesterol, and sugar. (24)

17. Maintain strict compliance with posttransplant medical treatment regimen, lifestyle changes, and necessary aftercare. (25, 26, 28, 29)

18. Report to appropriate health care professionals any physical symptoms that cause concern. (27, 28)

19. Verbalize increased knowledge of safe birth control methods and of medical risks associated with pre- or posttransplant pregnancy or childbirth. (30)

20. Acknowledge any disruption in sexual functioning and identify potential contributing factors. (31)

21. Verbally express emotions associated with medical condition, transplant surgery, and life changes caused by medical condition. (23, 32, 33, 34, 35)

22. Verbalize thoughts and fears about deterioration of health and dying. (35, 36)

23. Make a list of ongoing life stressors. (37)

medical treatment, such as faulty beliefs, unreasonable fears, educational or cognitive limitations, denial about severity of illness, financial constraints, or use of noncompliance as a form of "acting out."

10. Assess patient's current coping style in managing illness (e.g., active, problem-focused coping versus passive, avoidant coping).

11. Encourage patient to take an active role in implementing lifestyle changes, managing treatment regimen, and seeking information about medical condition and treatment.

12. Assess patient's social support network and availability of support members to assist with care before and after transplant.

13. Help patient identify, develop, and utilize support network to enhance coping with disease-related stressors and to implement lifestyle changes.

14. If patient will have to relocate to a new city for transplantation, clarify who will move with patient, and financial, residential, and vocational arrangements.

15. Provide family therapy to help family members address stressors associated with patient's medical condition (e.g., role and lifestyle changes, financial

24. Implement behavioral strategies to enhance ability to cope with and resolve external stressors. (15, 38)

25. Identify enjoyable activities and incorporate them into daily life. (39, 40)

26. Identify life goals and priorities and implement strategies to achieve goals. (41, 42)

27. Gradually resume daily activities following recovery from transplant surgery, following doctor's orders regarding physical restrictions and reporting any physical symptoms that cause concern. (29, 41, 42, 43)

28. Express feelings about physical limitations and need to rely on others for assistance and support. (44)

29. Utilize relaxation strategies to manage stress and anxiety. (45, 51)

30. Participate in systematic desensitization to reduce anxiety associated with invasive medical procedures. (45, 46)

31. Clarify desires regarding end-of-life medical care and use of life-support measures. (47)

32. Identify and challenge negatively biased, self-defeating cognitions. (48)

33. Implement positive self-talk that promotes health and healing. (49)

concerns, uncertainty about the future, difficulties associated with relocation to transplant center).

16. Use clinical interview and/or administration of psychological testing instruments to assess for presence of severe psychiatric disorder that may interfere with patient's ability to tolerate the stresses of transplant surgery and necessary long-term aftercare.

17. Assess patient for substance or alcohol abuse and refer for chemical dependency treatment if needed.

18. Implement smoking cessation strategies (see Cigarette Smoking chapter in this *Planner*) or refer patient for treatment of nicotine addiction.

19. Explore and address patient's anxiety associated with prolonged wait for donor organ, fear of dying while waiting for an organ, and/or preoccupation with position on transplant list.

20. Process patient's feelings of guilt about wishing for an organ and the necessity of someone else dying in order to obtain organ.

21. In the case of living donor organ transplant (e.g., for kidney transplantation or living related lung transplantation), process patient's thoughts and emotions about family

34. Verbalize an attitude of hope, peace, and joy that fights disease and promotes recovery. (49, 50, 51)

—. _____

    _____

—. _____

    _____

—. _____

    _____

member donating organ or tissue for patient.

22. Encourage patient to seek out other transplant candidates and recipients to gain support, obtain firsthand knowledge about transplant, and to share feelings and concerns.

23. Refer patient to a support group for transplant candidates.

24. Refer patient for nutritional counseling to help him/her achieve and maintain ideal weight and to become informed about appropriate dietary intake.

25. Following organ transplantation, review patient's understanding of treatment regimen and lifestyle changes, including immunosuppressant medications, physical therapy, dietary restrictions, physical limitations, and the need to avoid exposure to infection.

26. Assign patient to keep a written record of the name and dose of each prescribed medication, its potential side effects, and when and how to take it.

27. Encourage transplant recipient to monitor potential symptoms of infection or transplant rejection (e.g., fever, increased fatigue, generalized weakness, shortness of breath, nausea, vomiting, dizziness, faint-

ing) and to contact transplant coordinator if these
symptoms are experienced.

28. Monitor transplant recipient's attendance at medical,
dental, and opthalmological
appointments to maintain
optimal health and to en-
sure early detection of infection.

29. Monitor and reinforce patient's compliance with rehabilitation program (e.g.,
physical therapy, exercise).

30. Encourage patient to obtain
medical advice about risks
of pregnancy and childbirth
and about safe birth control
methods.

31. Explore and address factors
contributing to changes in
patient's sexual activity
(e.g., depression, loss of sexual desire, body image concerns, fatigue, medication
effects, fears, impotence).

32. Assess and treat concomitant anxiety and depres-
sion. (See Anxiety and
Depression chapters in this
Planner.) Explore factors
that contribute to anxious
or depressed mood.

33. Explore the emotional impact of life changes associated with patient's medical
condition and transplant
surgery.

34. Normalize and encourage
the expression of patient's
feelings of grief, anger, or
anxiety associated with

medical condition and the changes caused by it.

35. Assign patient to keep a daily journal of emotions to be shared in treatment sessions.

36. Process patient's fears about death and dying.

37. Ask patient to list current sources of stress, including illness symptoms, interpersonal stressors, lifestyle and role changes, and financial concerns.

38. Assist patient in developing coping strategies to address external stressors (e.g., problem solving, communication skills, assertiveness training).

39. Ask patient to complete the Inventory of Rewarding Activities (Birchler and Weiss, 1977) to help identify various desirable, pleasurable activities.

40. Help patient plan for the implementation of pleasurable activities to enhance life satisfaction.

41. Explore patient's goals, aspirations, and priorities with regard to social relationships, career, and personal growth. Determine whether goals are realistic and help patient develop a plan for reaching these goals.

42. Help patient explore options for return to work after transplant. Refer for

vocational counseling if indicated.

43. Address unreasonable fears
    and misconceptions that
    contribute to prolonged sick
    role behavior and avoidance
    of resuming responsibilities
    after recovery from trans-
    plant.

44. Process patient's fears
    about being dependent on
    others, of being a burden,
    and of loss of control.

45. Train patient in relaxation
    techniques (e.g., imagery,
    diaphragmatic breathing,
    deep-muscle relaxation) to
    reduce stress and tension
    and to promote a sense of
    peace and well-being.

46. Provide systematic desensi-
    tization to help patient re-
    duce anxiety associated
    with invasive medical pro-
    cedures.

47. Encourage patient to clarify
    with family members wishes
    about withdrawal of life
    support in the case of physi-
    cal decline.

48. Help patient identify irra-
    tional beliefs and negative
    cognitions about illness-
    related stressors.

49. Assist patient in developing
    positive, realistic, hopeful
    self-talk that promotes
    peace, good spirits, and
    healing.

50. Challenge patient to main-
    tain a positive, optimistic
    attitude to best create a

physiological, emotional, and spiritual atmosphere that will enhance healing powers and fight disease.

51. Teach patient to utilize visualization techniques to create positive images of adaptively coping with medical condition, medical/surgical procedures, and other life challenges.

__. _____

_____

__. _____

_____

__. _____

_____

DIAGNOSTIC SUGGESTIONS

Axis I:	316	Psychological Factors Affecting (Axis III Disorder)
	309.0	Adjustment Disorder with Depressed Mood
	309.24	Adjustment Disorder with Anxiety
	309.28	Adjustment Disorder with Mixed Anxiety and Depressed Mood
	293.89	Anxiety Disorder Due to (Axis III Disorder)
	V15.8	Noncompliance with Treatment
	_____	_____
	_____	_____

PREMENSTRUAL SYNDROME/ DYSPHORIC DISORDER (PMS/PDD)

BEHAVIORAL DEFINITIONS

1. Symptoms of depressed mood, tension, anxiety, emotional lability, irritability, anger, impaired concentration, food cravings, insomnia or hypersomnia, lethargy, breast tenderness, and/or bloating that are recurrently experienced during the week preceding onset of menstruation (PMS).
2. Diagnosis of premenstrual dysphoric disorder (PDD) as evidenced by cyclical recurrence of distressing affective, behavioral, and physical symptoms during the luteal phase of menstrual cycle for the past 12 months.
3. Premenstrual symptoms that significantly interfere with daily activities and/or negatively impact relationships with others.

__. _____
   _____
__. _____
   _____
   _____
__. _____
   _____

LONG-TERM GOALS

1. Recognize, accept, and cope with affective, behavioral, and somatic symptoms of premenstrual dysphoric disorder.
2. Alleviate depressive and anxiety symptoms and return to previous level of effective functioning.
3. Implement coping strategies to enhance emotional adaptation to life changes and ongoing stressors.

4. Implement positive health behaviors (e.g., exercise, proper diet, regular sleep-wake cycle, abstinence from drugs and alcohol) to enhance physical and mental health.

__. _____

_____

__. _____

_____

__. _____

_____

SHORT-TERM OBJECTIVES

1. Cooperate with a complete physical exam and develop a plan for follow-up medical care. (1)

2. Describe history of emotional and somatic symptoms, effects on daily functioning, and strategies used to resolve symptoms. (2, 3, 4)

3. Verbalize feelings of depression and associated signs and symptoms. (4)

4. Take antidepressant medication as prescribed and report any problems or side effects to therapist or physician. (5, 6)

5. Accurately complete rating forms of emotional and physical symptoms on each day of the menstrual cycle. (7, 8, 9)

6. Verbalize increased knowledge of premenstrual disorders, associated symptoms,

THERAPEUTIC INTERVENTIONS

1. Refer patient for physical exam, if she is not already under a physician's care.

2. Assess onset, duration, intensity, and course of patient's emotional and physical symptoms and their impact on her day-to-day living.

3. Explore strategies patient has utilized to resolve symptoms on her own and degree to which these efforts were successful.

4. Assess severity of depressive symptoms and provide interventions to address depression. (See Depression chapter in this *Planner*.)

5. Refer patient to a psychiatrist to assess the need for antidepressant medication.

6. Monitor patient's compliance with antidepressant medication and encourage her to report side effects or problems to physician.

and treatment options.
(1, 8, 10)

7. Engage in a regular exercise routine. (11)

8. Maintain a healthy diet, including appropriate intake of vegetables, fruits, carbohydrates, and proteins, with decreased intake of fat, cholesterol, caffeine, salt, and sugar. (12)

9. Develop routines to maximize sleep and rest and to maintain an appropriate sleep-wake cycle. (13, 14)

10. Terminate abuse of alcohol and/or illicit drugs. (15, 16)

11. Terminate use or abuse of nicotine. (15, 17)

12. Verbalize life circumstances that lead to worry, tension, or unhappiness. (18, 19)

13. Identify life circumstances that cannot be changed and must be coped with more effectively. (19)

14. Implement changes in life situation (e.g., vocational, marital, social, recreational) to reduce level of stress. (20, 22)

15. Identify and implement strategies to increase sense of control and self-confidence in coping with daily stressors. (21, 23, 24)

16. Verbalize insight into role of past traumatic experiences in contributing to current level of emotional distress. (25)

7. To assess patient for premenstrual dysphoric disorder, ask her to complete a daily symptom rating form over a two-month period, indicating day of menstrual cycle, severity of emotional and physical symptoms, significant life events, and use of alcohol, drugs, and medications.

8. Use patient's daily symptoms ratings to graph changes in symptoms as a function of her menstrual cycle; provide feedback as to whether symptoms appear to be related to menstrual cycle.

9. If patient's symptoms are not systematically related to menstrual cycle, explore and provide feedback about other potential contributing factors.

10. Educate patient regarding premenstrual dysphoric disorder (PDD) and premenstrual syndrome (PMS), and discuss importance of good health habits in reducing symptoms.

11. Encourage patient to engage in regular aerobic exercise to enhance physical health. Use goal setting and behavioral contracting to increase compliance.

12. Refer patient to a nutritionist or recommend a book on nutrition to educate about healthy eating habits.

17. Share with therapist any suicidal or homicidal urges. (26)

18. Report no longer having thoughts of harming self or others. (27)

19. Share and process emotions about life changes and current concerns at a women's support group. (28)

__. _____
   _____

__. _____
   _____

__. _____
   _____

13. Encourage patient to maintain a regular sleep-wake cycle.

14. Explore and address factors that are interfering with appropriate sleep patterns (e.g., depression, caffeine use, stress, poor sleep habits) and educate patient about proper sleep hygiene.

15. Educate patient about the effects of drugs, alcohol, and nicotine on her health and, if applicable, on the developing fetus.

16. Assess patient for abuse of alcohol, illicit drugs, or prescription medications and if necessary refer for treatment of chemical dependence.

17. Implement strategies to enhance patient's motivation to quit smoking and refer for or provide smoking cessation treatment. (See Cigarette Smoking chapter in this *Planner.*)

18. Assist patient in identifying sources of daily stress.

19. Help patient differentiate between stressors under her control that can be altered versus stressors that must be accepted and coped with more effectively.

20. Encourage and reinforce ongoing implementation of life changes that will reduce stress.

21. Teach patient coping strategies (e.g., problem solving,

time management, assertiveness, communication skills) to manage daily stressors.

22. Assist patient and her significant other in developing strategies to provide more equitable distribution of childcare and household responsibilities as needed.

23. Train patient in relaxation strategies (e.g., diaphragmatic breathing, deep-muscle relaxation, guided imagery) to manage stress and tension and to promote a sense of well-being.

24. Use modeling, role playing, and behavioral rehearsal to teach patient assertiveness skills to enhance effective communication of needs and concerns with partner, family, friends, colleagues, and health care professionals.

25. Explore patient's history of rape and/or sexual, emotional, and physical abuse. Help her achieve insight into how current events and circumstances may serve as cues to trigger memories and emotional reactions associated with previous abuse or trauma.

26. Assess patient for suicidal ideation and homicidal ideation and arrange for psychiatric hospitalization if she is a danger to self or others.

27. Reinforce positive statements regarding the future that reflect hopefulness and a sense of control over life circumstances.

28. Refer patient to a women's support or focus group.

__. _____
    _____

__. _____
    _____

__. _____
    _____

DIAGNOSTIC SUGGESTIONS

Axis I: 296.2x   Major Depressive Disorder, Single Episode
296.3x   Major Depressive Disorder, Recurrent
311   Depressive Disorder NOS
309.0   Adjustment Disorder with Depressed Mood
309.24   Adjustment Disorder with Anxiety
309.28   Adjustment Disorder with Mixed Anxiety and Depressed Mood
300.00   Anxiety Disorder NOS

_____   _____

_____   _____

PRESCRIPTION DRUG ABUSE/ DEPENDENCE

BEHAVIORAL DEFINITIONS

1. Consistent overuse of medication originally intended for control of medical symptoms.
2. Conflicts with physicians over type and amount of use of prescription drugs, often leading to "doctor shopping" for a source that will prescribe a specific drug or drugs.
3. Excessive worry about health and well-being when not taking medication.
4. Preoccupation with information about both prescription and nonprescription medications.
5. Reluctance to leave doctor's office without prescription.
6. Drug use to achieve mood alteration (Type A/Mood Altering dependency).
7. Drug use to prevent withdrawal symptoms (Type B/Iatrogenic dependency).
8. Drug-seeking for purpose of symptom relief, usually pain (Type C/Pseudo-addiction dependency).
9. Drug-seeking as symptom of somatization disorder (Type D/Somatization dependency).
10. Spends excessive money on both prescription and nonprescription medications.
11. High risk of physical complications from excessive drug use and/or from drug interactions from multiple medications.
12. Denial that physical or psychological dependency on a drug is a problem.
13. Increased tolerance for the drug as there is the need to use more to obtain the desired effect.
14. Physical withdrawal symptoms (i.e., shaking, seizures, nausea, headaches, sweating, anxiety, insomnia, and/or depression) when going without the addictive drug for any length of time.

___. _____
     _____
___. _____
     _____
___. _____
     _____

LONG-TERM GOALS

1. Clarify the nature of the drug-seeking pattern of behavior and then eliminate this self-destructive pattern.
2. If mood-altering type of dependency, actively participate in a recovery program leading to total abstinence.
3. If iatrogenic dependency, successfully follow a detoxification schedule if drug is no longer medically indicated, or develop a carefully regulated schedule of administration if drug is still appropriate.
4. If pseudo-addiction type of dependency, develop a safe and effective medication regimen appropriate to medical condition.
5. If drug dependence is based in somatization disorder, reduce the level of anxiety about health and the compulsive need to take medication.
6. Acquire the necessary skills to handle anxiety and other dysphoric moods without inappropriate reliance on drugs.
7. Develop the ability to use medications as prescribed.

___. _____
     _____
___. _____
     _____
___. _____
     _____

SHORT-TERM OBJECTIVES

1. Honestly describe history and current use of mood-altering substances and the motivation for drug-seeking behavior. (1, 2)

2. Become knowledgeable about different forms of drug dependency and honestly evaluate reasons for taking mood-altering drugs. (1, 2, 3)

3. Verbalize an acceptance of why doctors and family are concerned about perceived need for a high-risk type and amount of medication. (2, 4, 5)

4. Honestly identify the negative impact of medication/drug abuse on life. (1, 6)

5. Acknowledge that there is a real risk of developing physiologic and psychological dependency on illicit drugs or alcohol and on some medications that are legitimately prescribed for control of pain and disease symptoms. (4, 6, 7)

6. Eliminate the reaction that the doctor is not doing his/her job if an office visit does not lead to a prescription. (4, 5, 6, 7, 8)

7. Verbalize an understanding of the fact that there are differences of opinion among doctors regarding use of various medications,

THERAPEUTIC INTERVENTIONS

1. Obtain history of past and present prescription medication or illicit drug/alcohol use from patient and from medical/psychological history, assessing the type of drug dependency present.

2. Explore patient's attitudes and expectations regarding the use of mood-altering drugs; challenge assumption that there is a chemical solution for every incident of physical pain or emotional suffering.

3. Teach the patient about the four types of drug dependence (i.e., mood-altering, iatrogenic, pseudo-addiction, and somatization-based) and assist him/her in identifying the form he/she has.

4. Encourage the patient to consider why doctors may be reluctant to continue prescribing drugs that can be habit forming or have problematic side effects.

5. Engage patient in a discussion of how his/her perceived need for certain medication may be at odds with doctor's ethical obligation to do what is medically justified and therefore in patient's best interest.

6. Assign patient to list problems and conflicts caused by use/abuse of addictive drugs

especially medications for pain. (5, 8, 9, 10)

8. Eliminate most emergent behavior leading to poorly coordinated medication planning (e.g., ER visits, using other's medication, calling for prescription re-fills). (11)

9. Decrease the level of denial about drug dependence as evidenced by fewer state-ments downplaying amount of use and negative impact on life. (1, 6, 12)

10. Accept referral for treat-ment for drug dependency that is based in primarily seeking mood alteration. (13)

11. Ask doctor whether discon-tinuation of medication is likely to produce with-drawal symptoms. (7, 14)

12. Follow drug-tapering proto-col as required to eliminate physiologic dependency. (7, 13, 14)

13. Sign a contract that stipu-lates that use of medication will be strictly limited to prescription parameters. (15, 16, 21)

14. Accurately self-monitor all medication use. (16, 17)

15. Guard against accidental loss, theft, or destruction of medication to avoid prema-ture requests for refills that become a "red flag" to doc-tors. (16, 17)

and to process this informa-tion with therapist.

7. Determine whether pa-tient's pattern of drug use places him/her at risk for experiencing physiologic withdrawal symptoms if the drug is abruptly withdrawn.

8. Encourage open communi-cation between patient and primary care physician, al-lowing that physician to monitor all specialists' treatment and medications.

9. Obtain physician's assess-ment of patient's condition and recommended treat-ments.

10. Acknowledge patient's right to be treated fairly, but em-phasize that doctors and therapists have personal biases for or against the use of particular types of medi-cation.

11. Enlist patient's cooperation in setting firm limits on use of emergency treatment leading to prescriptions being given that are not part of a systematic treat-ment plan.

12. Confront patient's denial of drug dependence by review-ing such issues as drug tol-erance, negative impact of drugs on life, preoccupation with drug procurement, fear associated with being unable to access drugs, and irritability associated with withdrawal.

16. Inform all doctors and pharmacists of all prescription and nonprescription drugs that are being taken. (8, 11, 18)

17. Use medication only as prescribed and report benefits and problems to therapists and doctors. (11, 15, 16, 19)

18. Be open and honest with doctors and therapist about any past problems with chemical dependency. (1, 3, 8, 20)

19. Verbalize an understanding of the rationale and mutual responsibilities involved if physician or treatment program requires signing of a medication-use agreement. (15, 21)

20. Verbalize an understanding of situational, personality, social, and family factors that may foster chemical dependency. (22, 23, 24)

21. Verbalize how living situation contributes to chemical dependence and acts as a hindrance to recovery. (24, 25)

22. Identify alternatives to medication as primary form of health maintenance and/or pain relief. (26, 27, 28)

23. Identify negative, distorted thoughts that promote tension, fear, and increased pain. (29)

24. Implement positive, realistic self-talk as a means of reducing drug-seeking and

13. If Type A pattern of drug dependency, refer patient for or conduct chemical dependence treatment.

14. Refer patient to a physician to evaluate the need for and to administer a drug-tapering protocol to reduce withdrawal effects.

15. If narcotic use is medically justified, have patient sign narcotic use contract specifying agreement to use medication only as prescribed and to have medication prescribed by only one physician or treatment program.

16. Teach the patient to maintain careful self-monitoring records of medication use.

17. Insist on patient exercising great care in handling of all medications and point out consequence of carelessness resulting in loss, destruction, or incorrect use.

18. Direct patient to inform all doctors and pharmacists of all prescription and nonprescription drugs that are being consumed; monitor for follow-through.

19. Monitor patient's drug use, reviewing self-monitoring records and assessing for any abuse or side effects.

20. Urge patient to be open and honest with all treating physicians regarding history of illicit drug abuse and prescription abuse.

stress as well as increasing pain tolerance. (30)

25. Implement the use of relaxation and positive imagery as alternative coping strategies to pills and alcohol for controlling mood and energy level. (31, 32)

26. Exercise caution with over-the-counter medications and in mixing them with prescription medications. (33)

—. _____
_____

—. _____
_____

—. _____
_____

21. Explain the rationale for a signed contract regarding medication use and urge patient's cooperation with the procedure.

22. Assess patient's intellectual, personality, and cognitive functioning in relationship to their contribution to chemical dependence.

23. Probe patient's family history for chemical dependence patterns and relate these to patient's use.

24. Investigate situational stress factors beyond pain and illness that may foster patient's chemical dependence.

25. Encourage patient and family to question role of pills in treating personal as well as family tensions and unhappiness.

26. Teach patient alternatives (e.g., cognitive restructuring, diversion, relaxation skills, pain acceptance) to drug use/abuse as a means of dealing with emotional and/or physical pain.

27. Aid patient in understanding the integration of a cognitive-behavioral pain/illness management plan with appropriate medication use.

28. Raise patient's awareness of mind-body relationships.

29. Assist patient in identifying negative, distorted thoughts that foster tension, fear, and exacerbated pain.

30. Teach and reinforce positive realistic, cognitive self-talk as a means of coping with pain and emotional distress.

31. Instruct patient in how to use cognitive and somatic self-relaxation techniques (e.g., breath control, muscle relaxation, and visual imagery).

32. Provide patient with cassette tapes and written material for home practice of self-regulation skills.

33. Urge patient to consult with physician before consuming over-the-counter medications.

__. _____
_____

__. _____
_____

__. _____
_____

DIAGNOSTIC SUGGESTIONS

Axis I:	304.10	Sedative, Hypnotic, or Anxiolytic Dependence
	304.80	Polysubstance Dependence
	304.00	Opioid Dependence
	305.50	Opioid Abuse
	292.0	Opioid Withdrawal
	292.81	Opioid Intoxication Delirium
	300.81	Somatization Disorder
	V15.81	Noncompliance with Treatment
	304.30	Cannabis Dependence
	303.90	Alcohol Dependence
	_____	_____
	_____	_____

SICKLE-CELL DISEASE (SCD)

BEHAVIORAL DEFINITIONS

1. Ischemic tissue injury to all bodily systems (e.g., fever, chest pain, shortness of breath, increasing fatigue, abdominal swelling, unusual headache, sudden weakness or loss of feeling, painful erection, sudden vision changes).
2. Widespread chronic and acute pain.
3. Feelings of depression and anxiety due to disease and life disruption.
4. Reduced feelings of self-worth.
5. Impairments in cognitive and motor functioning.
6. Compromised social, academic, and vocational development.

__. _____
    _____
__. _____
    _____
    _____
__. _____
    _____

LONG-TERM GOALS

1. Minimize the physical and emotional effects of SCD as much as possible.
2. Acquire stress- and pain-management skills to enhance adaptation to disease.
3. Become as knowledgeable as possible about SCD and as self-reliant as possible in dealing with the disease.
4. Fully understand the inheritance pattern of SCD and seek genetic counseling if considering parenthood.

5. Know and practice the behaviors that can promote health, and reduce or eliminate behaviors that can increase risk of SCD episode.
6. Increase compliance with an adjustment to necessary medical procedures.
7. Decrease feelings of fear, anxiety, and helplessness.

—. _____

_____

—. _____

_____

—. _____

_____

SHORT-TERM OBJECTIVES

1. Describe how SCD is experienced and the impact it has had on all aspects of life. (1)
2. Verbalize accurate information about the genetics, symptoms, and regulation of SCD. (2)
3. Verbally express fears about episodic and potential long-term deterioration of physical condition. (3, 4)
4. Identify and verbally express feelings of depression or anxiety about medical condition and its effects on daily living. (4, 5)
5. Establish trusting relationship with a physician knowledgeable about SCD. (6, 7)
6. Assertively ask clear questions and report any physical symptoms to those

THERAPEUTIC INTERVENTIONS

1. Explore symptoms and severity of SCD in patient, as well as how SCD has affected his/her daily living.
2. Explore patient's understanding of SCD; assisting him/her in obtaining SCD information from sources such as health care professionals, books, and reputable Internet sites.
3. Explore and process patient's fears associated with deterioration of physical health.
4. Normalize patient's feelings of grief, sadness, or anxiety associated with medical condition and encourage verbal expression of these emotions.
5. Process patient's feelings of grief and frustration associated with disruption of lifestyle.

people involved in managing medical treatment. (7, 8, 9)

7. Comply with medication regimen and necessary medical procedures, reporting any side effects to physician. (8, 9, 10, 11)

8. If pain is a significant symptom, verbalize an awareness of the potential for developing analgesic drug tolerance and/or dependency. (12, 13)

9. Verbalize a plan for dealing with an SCD emergency that might be precipitated by any change in life circumstances. (13, 14)

10. Describe the pattern of narcotic medication, alcohol, and nicotine use or abuse. (15)

11. Terminate the use of alcohol and/or nicotine and the abuse of any narcotics or street drugs. (15, 16)

12. Verbalize an understanding and acceptance of the implications of what it means to have, or be a carrier of, a genetically transmitted disease; seek genetic counseling and advice. (2, 17, 18, 19, 20)

13. Parents/caretaker verbalize confidence in ability to monitor health of SCD infant or child, seeking immediate medical attention if child shows signs of infections or onset of sickle-cell episode. (9, 21, 22, 23)

6. Consult with patient's physician and other pertinent medical personnel to enhance coordination of medical and psychological treatments.

7. Encourage and role play the patient asking clear questions of those people involved in medical care and support.

8. Challenge patient passivity; reward active participation in all aspects of disease management.

9. Assist patient and/or significant others in monitoring physical symptoms that require medical attention, and review the necessary steps to obtain appropriate medical care.

10. Explore and address misconceptions, fears, and situational factors that interfere with patient's compliance with medical treatment.

11. Gently confront patient's denial of the seriousness of condition and stress need for compliance with medical treatment procedures.

12. Present risks and benefits of using narcotic medication for pain control, encouraging client to carefully monitor narcotic use and recognize and report signs of tolerance and dependency.

13. Review with patient pain treatment options.

14. Parents/caretaker verbalize a balance of health concerns while encouraging normal development of SCD child. (21, 24)

15. Regularly drink recommended amount of water, get sufficient rest, exercise as appropriate, avoid extreme temperatures and extreme exertion. (25)

16. Attend an SCD support group or parent support group. (26)

17. Verbalize life circumstances that lead to worry, tension, or stress. (27)

18. Acknowledge the negative effect stress has on SCD flare-ups. (28, 29)

19. Identify and reduce those sources of external stress that can reasonably be changed or avoided. (30, 31)

20. Attend personal, vocational, and marital/family counseling sessions to reduce stress in those areas. (31)

21. List educational, vocational, and social interests and goals; avoid allowing the disease to become the primary focus of personal identity. (31, 32)

22. Identify distorted cognitions in response to daily events and illness-related stressors that contribute to anxiety or depression. (33, 34)

23. Increase use of positive self-talk in response to symptoms or other sources of stress. (35)

14. Review with patient plans for dealing with possible SCD emergency as part of coping plan for any change in life circumstances (e.g., prior to moving, starting new job, taking a trip).

15. Assess patient's use or abuse of narcotic medications and/or alcohol to control pain; refer for substance abuse/dependency treatment if necessary.

16. Teach patient the deleterious effects of the use of alcohol and nicotine as they interact with SCD and its treatment.

17. Explain to patient and family the genetics of SCD, including difference between sickle-cell trait and sickle-cell disease.

18. Explore patient's feelings about having a genetically transmitted disease; reinforce responsible actions regarding future generations.

19. Encourage all members of the patient's family to be tested for sickle-cell trait.

20. Encourage the use of genetic counseling if patient is planning to have children.

21. Explore patient's support system, determining who is available to help with behavioral compliance to disease requirements.

22. Support parent/caretaker of SCD child in developing

24. Implement the use of mental imagery and psychophysiological self-relaxation skills involving breath control and muscle relaxation to manage pain and stress. (36, 37)

25. Learn and use the cognitive self-analgesia of focusing attention on pleasant distracting images and sensations to inhibit discomfort. (36, 37, 38)

26. Strive to develop adaptive philosophic and spiritual attitudes toward disease, pain, and suffering as sometimes being a necessary part of living. (35, 39)

27. Verbalize an attitude of hope, peace, and joy that helps resist disease process. (35, 39)

—. _____

_____

—. _____

_____

—. _____

_____

confidence in capacity to monitor child's symptoms and respond appropriately.

23. Take necessary action (e.g., report to Protective Services, Public Health, and/or client's personal physician) to protect child from ravages of poor SCD management if the family of the child is unable or unwilling to provide adequate care and supervision.

24. Help parents/caretaker to focus on normal child development issues and not exclusively on disease concerns.

25. Review and reinforce health-related behaviors (e.g., sufficient rest, appropriate exercise, drinking recommended amount of water daily, avoiding extreme temperature changes and exertion) specific to SCD and to health in general.

26. Help the patient or the parents/caretaker of child-aged patient find a support group and encourage attendance; process reactions to the meetings.

27. Explore stresses that patient is facing in daily life.

28. Raise patient's awareness of mind-body relationships.

29. Teach patient about the possible effects of stress on SCD episodes.

30. Aid patient in recognizing sources of environmental stress (versus internal stress) and in reducing those that can be modified.

31. Encourage patient's use of personal, vocational, and marital/family counseling, and make referrals as needed.

32. Help patient and/or family develop strategies for maintaining focus on educational, vocational, and socialization goals despite time lost to disease episodes, discouraging gravitating to "disability" as the primary focus of client's life.

33. Encourage patient in recognizing dysfunctional automatic thoughts and emotional response patterns that may contribute to high levels of stress.

34. Assess the severity of patient's depression and anxiety, and treat if necessary. (See Depression and Anxiety chapters in this *Planner.*)

35. Teach and reinforce patient's use of positive, realistic cognitive self-talk as a means of coping with internal stress.

36. Instruct patient in how to use cognitive and somatic self-relaxation techniques such as breath control, muscle relaxation, and visual imagery.

37. Provide patient with cassette tapes and written material for home practice of self-regulation skills.

38. Teach patient how to move from self-relaxation to use of imagery analgesia.

39. Facilitate talk about feelings of injustice and discrimination in all aspects of patient's life; encourage a positive perspective that includes acceptance and forgiveness balanced with assertiveness and fairness.

__. _____

_____

__. _____

_____

__. _____

_____

DIAGNOSTIC SUGGESTIONS

Axis I: 316   Psychological Factors Affecting Sickle-Cell Disease
              307.89   Pain Disorder Associated with Both Psychological Factors and Sickle-Cell Disease
              309.0   Adjustment Disorder with Depressed Mood
              304.80   Polysubstance Dependence
              _____   _____
              _____   _____

Appendix A

BIBLIOTHERAPY SUGGESTIONS

Acute Pain

Cowles, J. (1993). *Pain relief! How to say "no" to acute, chronic, and cancer pain.* New York: Mastermedia Limited.

Fanning, P. (1992). *Visualization for healing injuries.* Oakland, CA: New Harbinger Press.

Anxiety Related to Medical Problems

Benson, H. (1975). *The relaxation response.* New York: William Morrow.

Burns, D. (1993). *Ten days to self-esteem.* New York: Morrow.

Craske, M., & Barlow, D. (1994). *Mastering your anxiety and worry—Patients workbook.* San Antonio, TX: The Psychological Corporation.

Davis, M., Eshelman, E., & McKay, M. (1988). *The relaxation and stress reduction workbook.* Oakland, CA: New Harbinger.

Hauck, Paul. (1975). *Overcoming worry and fear.* Philadelphia, PA: Westminster Press.

Marks, Isaac. (1980). *Living with fear: Understanding and coping with anxiety.* New York: McGraw-Hill.

Arthritis

Arthritis Foundation. (1997). *Arthritis 101: Questions you have, answers you need.* Marietta, GA: Longstreet Press.

Fries, J. F. (1995). *Arthritis: A take care of yourself health guide for understanding arthritis* (4th ed.). Portland, OR: Perseus Press.

Gordon, N. F., & Cooper, K. H. (1992). *Arthritis: Your complete exercise guide.* (Cooper Clinic and Research Institute Fitness Series.) Champaign, IL: Human Kinetics Publishing.

Lorig, K. (Ed.). (1994). *Living a healthy life with chronic conditions: Self-management of heart disease, arthritis, stroke, diabetes, asthma, bronchitis, emphysema and others.* Menlo Park, CA: Bull Publishing Co.

Lorig, K., & Fries, J. F. (1996). *The arthritis helpbook: A tested self-management program for coping with arthritis and fibromyalgia.* Portland, OR: Perseus Press.

Asthma

Freedman, M. R., Rosenberg, S. J., & Divino, C. L. (1998). *Living well with asthma.* New York: Guilford Press.

Rooklin, A. R., & Masline, S. R. (1995). *Living with asthma.* New York: Plume.

Sander, N. (1994). *A parent's guide to asthma.* New York: Plume.

Cancer

Canfield, J., Hansen, M. V., Aubery, P. & Mitchell, N. (1996). *Chicken soup for the surviving soul.* Deerfield Beach, FL: Health Communications, Inc.

Cousins, N. (1990). *Head first: The biology of hope and the healing power of the human spirit.* New York: Penguin.

Cousins, N. & Dubos, R. (1995). *Anatomy of an illness as perceived by the patient: Reflections on healing and regeneration.* New York: W. W. Norton.

Cunningham, A. (1989). *Helping yourself: A workbook for people living with cancer.* Toronto: Ontario Cancer Institute.

Hersch, S. P. (1998). *Beyond miracles: Living with cancer.* Chicago: Contemporary Books.

Johnson, J., & Klein, L. (1994). *I can cope: Staying healthy with cancer.* Minneapolis, MN: Chronimed Publishing.

Landro, L. (1998). *Survivor: Taking control of your fight against cancer.* New York: Simon & Schuster.

LeShan, L. (1977). *You can fight for your life.* New York: M. Evans and Company.

Siegel, B. (1986). *Love, medicine, and miracles.* New York: Harper and Row.

———. (1989). *Peace, love, and healing.* New York: Harper and Row.

Cardiovascular Disease

Friedman, M., and Olmer, D. (1984). *Treating type A behaviors and your heart.* New York: Alfred Knopf.

Maximin, A., Stevic-Rust, L., & Kenyon, L. W. (1997). *Heart therapy: Regaining your cardiac health.* Oakland, CA: New Harbinger.

Williams, R. (1989). *The trusting heart: Great news about Type A behavior.* New York: Times Books.

Robinson, B. (1993). *Overdoing it.* Deerfield Beach, FL: Health Communications, Inc.

Chronic Fatigue Syndrome (CFS)

Bell, D. S. (1995). *The doctor's guide to chronic fatigue syndrome: Understanding, treating, and living with CFS.* Portland, OR: Perseus Press.

Fisher, G. C., Cheney, P. R. & Oleske, J. M. (1997). *Chronic fatigue syndrome: A comprehensive guide to symptoms, treatments, and solving the practical problems of CFS.* New York: Warner Books.

Friedberg, F. (1996). *Coping with chronic fatigue syndrome: Nine things you can do.* Oakland, CA: New Harbinger Press.

Jacobs, G. (1998). *Chronic fatigue syndrome: A comprehensive guide to effective treatment.* ("The Natural Way" Series.) Roslyn, NY: Berrent.

Chronic Obstructive Pulmonary Disorder (COPD)

Adams, F. V. (1998). *The breathing disorders sourcebook.* Los Angeles, CA: Lowell House.

Haas, F., Haas, S. S. & Axen, K. (1990). *The chronic bronchitis and emphysema handbook.* New York: John Wiley & Sons.

Smolley, L. A., & Bruce, D. F. (1998). *Breathe right now.* New York: W. W. Norton & Company.

Chronic Pain

Catalano, E. M., & Hardin, K. N. (1996). *The chronic pain control workbook: A step-by-step guide for coping with and overcoming pain.* Oakland, CA: New Harbinger Press.

Caudill, M. A. (1995). *Managing pain before it manages you.* New York: Guilford Publications.

Jamison, R. N. (1996). *Learning to master your chronic pain.* Sarasota, FL: Professional Resource Press.

Sternbach, R. A. (1995). *Mastering pain: A twelve-step program for coping with chronic pain.* New York: Ballantine Books.

Cigarette Smoking

Burton, D. (1986). *American Cancer Society's "freshstart": 21 days to stop smoking.* New York: Pocket Books.

Fisher, E. B. (1998). *American Lung Association: Seven steps to a smoke-free life.* New York: John Wiley & Sons.

Rustin, T. A. (1996). *Keep quit! A motivational guide to a life without smoking.* Center City, MN: Hazelden.

Stevic-Rust, L. (1996). *The stop smoking workbook.* Oakland, CA: New Harbinger.

Cystic Fibrosis (CF)

Orenstein, D. M. (1996). *Cystic fibrosis: A guide for patient and family.* Haggerstown, MD: Lippincott-Raven Publishers.

Shapiro, B. L., & Huessner, R. C. (1991). *A patient's guide to cystic fibrosis.* Minneapolis, MN: University of Minnesota Press.

Dental Problems

Bourne, E. J. (1998). *The anxiety and phobia workbook.* Ravensdale, WA: Idyll Arbor, Inc.

Gold, M. (1988). *The good news about panic, anxiety, and phobias.* New York: Villard/Random House.

Kroeger, R. F. (1988). *How to overcome fear of dentistry.* Cincinnati, OH: Heritage Communications.

Wright, R. (1997). *Tough questions, great answers: Responding to patient concerns about today's dentistry.* Carol Stream, IL: Quintessence Publishing Co.

Depression Related to Medical Problems

Burns, D. (1980). *Feeling good: The new mood therapy.* New York: Signet.

————. (1989). *The feeling good handbook.* New York: Plume.

Frankl, V. (1959). *Man's search for meaning.* New York: Simon & Schuster.

Hallinan, P. K. (1976). *One day at a time.* Minneapolis, MN: CompCare.

Knauth, P. (1977). *A season in hell.* New York: Pocket Books.

Leith, L. (1998). *Exercising your way to better mental health.* Morgantown, WV: Fitness Information Technology, Inc.

Diabetes

American Diabetes Association. (1997). *American Diabetes Association complete guide to diabetes: The ultimate home diabetes reference.* New York: Bantam Books.

Fromer, M. J. (1998). *Healthy living with diabetes.* Oakland, CA: New Harbinger Press.

Schade, D. S. (Ed.). (1996). *101 tips for improving your blood sugar: A project of the American Diabetes Association.* Chicago, IL: Contemporary Books.

Tonnessen, D. (1996). *50 essential things to do when the doctor says it's diabetes.* New York: Plume Books.

Epilepsy

Browne, T. R., & Holmes, G. L. (1997). *Handbook of epilepsy.* Philadelphia, PA: Lippincott-Raven Publishers.

Freeman, J. M., Vining, E. P., and Pillas, D. J. (1997). *Seizures and epilepsy in childhood: A guide for parents.* Baltimore, MD: John Hopkins University Press.
Richard, A., & Reiter, J. (1995). *Epilepsy: A new approach.* New York: Walker & Company.

Fibromyalgia

Starlanyl, D. J. (1998). *The fibromyalgia advocate: Getting the support you need to cope with fibromyalgia and myofascial pain syndrome.* Oakland, CA: New Harbinger Press.
Starlanyl, D. J., and Copeland, M. E. (1996). *Fibromyalgia and chronic myofascial pain syndrome: A survival manual.* Oakland, CA: New Harbinger Press.
Williamson, M. E. (1996). *Fibromyalgia: A comprehensive approach: What you can do about chronic pain and fatigue.* New York: Walker & Company.

Gynecological and Obstetric Conditions

Cherry, S. H., & Runowicz, C. D. (1994). *The menopause book.* New York: Macmillan.
Dunnewold, A., and Sanford, D. G. (1994). *Postpartum survival guide.* Oakland, CA: New Harbinger.
Harkness, C. (1992). *The infertility book: A comprehensive medical and emotional guide.* Berkeley, CA: Celestial Arts.
Huysman, A. M. (1998). *A mother's tears: Understanding the mood swings that follow childbirth.* New York: Seven Stories Press.
Kleiman, K. R., & Raskin, V. D. (1994). *This isn't what I expected: Recognizing and recovering from depression and anxiety after childbirth.* New York: Bantam Books.
Landau, C., Cyr, M. G. & Moulton, A. W. (1994). *The complete book of menopause.* New York: Perigee.

Headache

DeGood, D. E. (1997). *The headache and neck pain workbook: An integrated mind and body program.* Oakland, CA: New Harbinger Press.
Duckro, P. N., Richardson, W. D. & Marshall, J. E. (1995). *Taking control of your headaches.* New York: Guilford Publications.
Rapoport, A. M., & Sheftell, F. D. (1990). *Headache relief.* New York: Simon & Schuster.
Saper, J. R., and K. Magee. (1986). *Freedom from headaches.* New York: Simon & Schuster.

HIV/AIDS

de Solla Price, M. (1995). *Living positively in a world with HIV/AIDS*. New York: Avon Books.

Eidson, T. (1993). *The AIDS caregiver's handbook*. New York: St. Martin's Press.

Franklin, L. R., & Leonard, J. M. (1997). *Questions and answers on AIDS*. Los Angeles, CA: Health Information Press.

Kubler-Ross, E. (1997). *AIDS: The ultimate challenge*. New York: Macmillan.

Irritable Bowel Syndrome (IBS)

Nicol, R., & Snape, W. (1995). *Irritable bowel syndrome: A natural approach*. Berkeley, CA: Ulysses Press.

Potterton, D. (1996). *All about irritable bowel syndrome; and its treatment without drugs*. UK: Foulsham & Co Ltd. (Distributed by Associated Pubs. Group, Nashville, TN.)

Scanlon, D., & Becnel, B. C. (1991). *The wellness book of I.B.S.: How to achieve relief from irritable bowel syndrome and live a symptom-free life*. New York: St. Martin's Press.

Shimberg, E. F. (1991). *Relief from IBS: Irritable bowel syndrome*. New York: Ballantine Books.

Multiple Sclerosis (MS)

Holland, N. J., Murray, R. J., & Reingold, S. C. (1996). *Multiple sclerosis: A guide for the newly diagnosed*. New York: Demos Vermande.

Schapiro, R. T. (1994). *Symptoms management in multiple sclerosis*. New York: Demos Vermande.

Shuman, R., Schwartz, J., & Slater, R. (1994). *Living with multiple sclerosis: A handbook for families*. New York: Macmillan.

Obesity

Beasley, J. D., & Knightley, S. (1994). *Food for recovery*. New York: Crown.

Brandon, C. W. (1993). *Am I hungry . . . Or am I hurting?* San Diego, CA: Recovery.

Fairburn, C. (1995). *Overcoming binge eating*. New York: Guilford Press.

Greeson, J. (1990). *It's not what you're eating, it's what's eating you*. New York: Pocket Books.

Kolodny, N. J. (1992). *When food's a foe*. Boston, MA: Little, Brown.

Roth, G. (1993). *Breaking free from compulsive eating*. New York: Plume.

Organ Transplantation

Cousins, N. (1990). *Head first: The biology of hope and the healing power of the human spirit.* New York: Penguin.

Cousins, N., & Dubos, R. (1995). *Anatomy of illness as perceived by the patient: Reflections on healing and regeneration.* New York: W. W. Norton.

Massachusetts General Hospital Organ Transplant Team, & Pizer, H. F. (1991). *Organ transplant: A patient's guide.* Boston, MA: Harvard University Press.

Siegel, B. (1989). *Peace, love, and healing.* New York: Harper and Row.

Premenstrual Syndrome/Dysphoric Disorder (PMS/PDD)

Lark, S. M. (1989). *Premenstrual syndrome self-help book: A woman's guide to feeling good all month.* Berkeley, CA: Celestial Arts.

Futterman, L. & Jones, J. (1997). *PMS sourcebook.* New York: Lowell House.

Prescription Drug Abuse/Dependence

Fanning, P., & O'Neill, J. T. (1996). *The addiction workbook: A step-by-step guide to quitting alcohol and drugs.* Oakland, CA: New Harbinger Press.

Kuhn, C., Swartzwelder, S., Wilson, W., Foster, J., & Wilson, L. W. (1998). *Buzzed: The straight facts about the most used and abused drugs from alcohol to ecstasy.* New York: W. W. Norton & Company.

O'Neill, J., & O'Neill, P. (1992). *Concerned intervention: When your loved one won't quit alcohol or drugs.* Oakland, CA: New Harbinger Press.

Schuckit, M. A. (1998). *Educating yourself about alcohol and drugs: A people's primer.* New York: Plenum Press.

Sickle-Cell Disease (SCD)

Beshore, G. W. (1994). *Sickle cell anemia.* Danbury, CT: Franklin Watts Inc.

Bloom, M. (1995). *Understanding sickle cell disease.* Jackson, MS: University Press of Mississippi.

Gordon, M. A. (1998). *Let's talk sickle cell anemia* (The Let's Talk Library). New York: Rosen Publishing Group.

Appendix B

INDEX OF DSM-IV CODES ASSOCIATED WITH PRESENTING PROBLEMS

Acute Stress Disorder   **308.3**
  Acute Pain
  Dental-Related Problems

**Adjustment Disorder
with Anxiety**   **309.24**
  Anxiety Related to Medical Problems
  Asthma
  Cancer
  Cardiovascular Disease
  Chronic Obstructive Pulmonary
    Disease (COPD)
  Cystic Fibrosis (CF)
  Diabetes
  Gynecological and Obstetric
    Conditions
  HIV/AIDS
  Organ Transplantation
  Premenstrual Syndrome/Dysphoric
    Disorder (PMS / PDD)

**Adjustment Disorder
with Depressed Mood**   **309.0**
  Cancer
  Cardiovascular Disease
  Chronic Obstructive Pulmonary
    Disease (COPD)
  Cystic Fibrosis (CF)
  Depression Related to Medical
    Problems
  Diabetes
  Gynecological and Obstetric
    Conditions
  HIV/AIDS

  Organ Transplantation
  Premenstrual Syndrome/Dysphoric
    Disorder (PMS / PDD)
  Sickle-Cell Disease (SCD)

**Adjustment Disorders with
Disturbance of Conduct**   **309.3**
  Diabetes
  HIV/AIDS

**Adjustment Disorder with
Mixed Anxiety and
Depressed Mood**   **309.28**
  Asthma
  Cancer
  Cardiovascular Disease
  Chronic Obstructive Pulmonary
    Disease (COPD)
  Cystic Fibrosis (CF)
  Fibromyalgia
  Gynecological and Obstetric
    Conditions
  HIV/AIDS
  Organ Transplantation
  Premenstrual Syndrome/Dysphoric
    Disorder (PMS / PDD)

Alcohol Dependence   **303.90**
  Prescription Drug Abuse/Dependence

**Amnestic Disorder Due to ...
(Axis III Disorder)**   **294.0**
  Epilepsy

Appendix C

BIBLIOGRAPHY

Blechman, E.A., & Brownell, K.D. (1997). *Behavioral medicine and women: A comprehensive handbook.* New York: Guilford Press.

Brigham, D.D., Davis, A., & Cameron-Sampey, D. (1994). *Imagery for getting well: Clinical applications in behavioral medicine.* New York: W.W. Norton & Co.

Camic, P.M., & Knight, S.J. (Eds.). (1998). *Clinical handbook of health psychology: A practical guide to effective interventions.* Seattle, WA: Hognefe and Huber.

Carlson, J.C., Seifert, A.R., & Birbaumer, N. (Eds.). (1994). *Clinical applied psychophysiology.* New York: Plenum.

Fairburn, C.G., & Wilson, G.T. (Eds.). (1993). *Binge eating: Nature, assessment, and treatment.* New York: Guilford Press.

Gatchel, R.J., & Blanchard, E.B. (Eds.). (1993). *Psychophysiological disorders: Research and clinical applications.* Washington, DC: American Psychological Association.

Gatchel, R.J., & Turk, D.C. (Eds.). (1996). *Psychological approaches to pain management: A practitioner's handbook.* New York: Guilford Press.

Jamison, R.N. (1996). *Mastering chronic pain: A professional's guide to behavioral treatment.* Sarasota, FL: Professional Resource Press.

Jongsma, A.E., & Peterson, L.M. (1999). *The complete adult psychotherapy treatment planner.* New York: John Wiley & Sons.

Kalichman, S.C. (1995). *Understanding AIDS: A guide for mental health professionals.* Washington, DC: American Psychological Association.

Sanders, S. (1991). *Clinical self-hypnosis: The power of words and images.* New York: Guilford Press.

Smith, T.W., & Leon, A.S. (1992). *Coronary heart disease: A behavioral perspective.* Champaign, IL: Research Press.

Spira, J.L. (Ed.). (1997). *Group therapy for medically ill patients.* New York: Guilford Press.

Practice Planners™ offer mental health professionals a full array of practice management tools. These easy-to-use resources include *Treatment Planners*, which cover

Practice *Planners*™

all the necessary elements for developing formal treatment plans, including detailed problem definitions, long-term goals, short-term objectives, therapeutic interventions, and DSM-IV diagnoses; *Homework Planners* featuring behaviorally-based, ready-to-use assignments which are designed for use between sessions; and *Documentation Sourcebooks* that provide all the forms and records that therapists need to run their practice.

For more information on the titles listed below, fill out and return this form to: John Wiley & Sons, Attn: M.Fellin, 605 Third Avenue, New York, NY 10158.

Name _____

Address _____

Address _____

City/State/Zip _____

Telephone _____ Email _____

Please send me more information on:

- ❏ The Child and Adolescent Psychotherapy Treatment Planner / 240pp / 0-471-15647-7 / $39.95
- ❏ The Chemical Dependence Treatment Planner / 208pp / 0-471-23795-7 / $39.95
- ❏ The Continuum of Care Treatment Planner / 208pp / 0-471-19568-5 / $39.95
- ❏ The Couples Therapy Treatment Planner / 208pp / 0-471-24711-1 / $39.95
- ❏ The Employee Assistance (EAP) Treatment Planner / 176pp / 0-471-24709-X / $39.95
- ❏ The Pastoral Counseling Treatment Planner / 208pp / 0-471-25416-9 / $39.95
- ❏ The Older Adult Psychotherapy Treatment Planner / 176pp / 0-471-29574-4 / $39.95
- ❏ The Group Therapy Treatment Planner / 176pp / 0-471-25469-X/ $39.95
- ❏ The Complete Adult Psychotherapy Treatment Planner, Second Edition / 224pp / 0-471-31922-4 / $39.95
- ❏ The Brief Couples Therapy Homework Planner / 224pp / 0-471-29511-6 / $49.95
- ❏ The Brief Therapy Homework Planner / 256pp / 0-471-24611-5 / $49.95
- ❏ The Chemical Dependence Treatment Homework Planner / 300pp / 0-471-32452-3 / $49.95
- ❏ The Adolescent Homework Planner / 256pp / 0-471-34465-6 / $49.95
- ❏ The Child Homework Planner / 256pp / 0-471-32366-7 / $49.95
- ❏ The Couples & Family Clinical Documentation Sourcebook / 208pp / 0-471-25234-4 / $49.95
- ❏ The Psychotherapy Documentation Primer / 224pp / 0-471-28990-6 / $39.95
- ❏ The Clinical Documentation Sourcebook / 256pp / 0-471-17934-5 / $49.95
- ❏ The The Forensic Documentation Sourcebook / 224pp / 0-471-25459-2 / $75.00
- ❏ The Chemical Dependence Treatment Documentation Sourcebook / 304pp / 0-471-31285-1 / $49.95
- ❏ The Child Clinical Documentation Sourcebook / 256pp / 0-471-29111-0 / $49.95

Order the above products through your local bookseller, or by calling 1-800-225-5945, from 8:30 a.m. to 5:30 p.m., EST. You can also order via our web site: www.wiley.com/practiceplanners

WILEY
Publishers Since 1807

TheraScribe® 3.0 for Windows®

The Computerized Assistant to Psychotherapy Treatment Planning

TheraBiller with TheraScheduler™

The Computerized Mental Health Office Manager

TheraBiller w/TheraScheduler™ is our new Windows®-based software package designed specifically to help you manage your mental health practice....

Powerful...
- TheraBiller™ with TheraScheduler™ integrates seamlessly with TheraScribe® 3.0: The Computerized Assistant to Psychotherapy Treatment Planning. Although each program can be used independently, by using them in cooperatively you'll get a complete office management system, with automatic common data sharing and one-button toggling
- Completes pre-printed or program-generated HCFA forms, and produces easy-to-read, professional-looking invoices and aged accounts receivable reports
- Tracks managed care information (sessions authorized, sessions used, capitated fees, hourly fees, etc.)
- Built-in electronic billing compatibility (claims module interfaces with the **MedE America Network**)
- Electronic cardex which prints mailing labels and tracks contact information

Flexible...
- Robust reporting options — print or preview billing summaries and usage statistics by provider, patient, or time-frame
- Full quick-reference DSM-IV and CPT code libraries (including new G-codes)
- Data export to Quicken® and MicroSoft Money®, as well as common spreadsheet and accounting programs (e.g., Excel®, Peachtree®, etc.)
- Perfect for solo providers or large group practices (the stand-alone version handles an unlimited number of providers, and a network version is also available)

User-Friendly...
- Features the same intuitive interface as Wiley's best-selling TheraScribe ®3.0.
- Includes a handy Billing Wizard to guide you through the billing process and a Report Wizard that helps you select report parameters
- Built-in appointment book, with daily, weekly, monthly scheduling for an unlimited number of providers— updates automatically when you book a session in TheraScribe® 3.0
- Password-protected to safeguard confidential data. Varying levels of data access may be assigned to each user

---

System Requirements
IBM®-compatible 486DX * 8 MB RAM (12MB recommended) * 10MB Hard Disk Space
VGA display (SVGA recommended) * Windows® 3.1

For more information on *TheraBiller*™, fill in this coupon, and mail it to: M. Fellin, John Wiley & Sons, Inc., 605 Third Avenue, New York, NY 10158.

Name _____

Affiliation _____

Address _____

City/State/Zip _____

Phone _____

Visit our web site and download a free demo: www.wiley.com/therabiller

WILEY
Publishers Since 1807

ABOUT THE DISK*

TheraScribe® 3.0 Library Module Installation

The enclosed disk contains files to upgrade your TheraScribe® 3.0 program to include the behavioral definitions, goals, objectives, interventions, and diagnoses from *The Behavioral Medicine Treatment Planner.*

Note: You must have TheraScribe® 3.0 for Windows installed on your computer to use *The Behavioral Medicine Treatment Planner* library module.

To install the library module, please follow these steps:

1. Place the library module disk in your floppy drive.
2. Log in to TheraScribe® 3.0 as the Administrator using the name "Admin" and your administrator password.
3. On the Main Menu, press the "GoTo" button, and choose the Options menu item.
4. Press the "Import Library" button.
5. On the Import Library Module screen, choose your floppy disk drive a:\ from the list and press "Go." Note: It may take a few minutes to import the data from the floppy disk to your computer's hard disk.
6. When the installation is complete, the library module data will be available in your TheraScribe® 3.0 program.

Note: If you have a network version of TheraScribe® 3.0 installed, you should import the library module one time only. After importing the data, the library module data will be available to all network users.

User Assistance

If you need assistance using this TheraScribe® 3.0 add-on module, contact Wiley Technical Support at:

Phone: 212-850-6753
Fax: 212-850-6800 (Attention: Wiley Technical Support)
E-mail: techhelp@wiley.com

---

*Note: This section applies only to the book with disk edition, ISBN 0-471-31926-0.

For information on how to install disk, refer to the **About the Disk** section on page 225.

WILEY

Publishers Since 1807